Finally!
What every good parent has been
A "How To" Manual Showing Parents How to Help Their Child
Become All He or She Can Be.

All children have the potential to be Top Students! Parents are their most important teachers, yet they have no training for their responsibilities. Kathleen teaches parents how to prepare their preschool child for formal learning just during their daily contact and child rearing and how to recognize learning opportunities, whether in the kitchen, backyard, car, the grocery store, (or virtually anywhere). She presents ideas and suggestions in an easy-to-follow format that allows working, stay-at-home, or home-school parents to weave as much as they are able into their busy schedule. Much learning is incorporated into games, art, and fun activities that keep the kids away from television and happily busy for hours.

Top Students / Top Parents is truly a must-have manual for all parents, teachers, and child care providers

TOP STUDENTS, TOP PARENTS

A Manual for Parents Who Want to Help Their Children
Become All They Can Be

KATHLEEN BURNS
MOTHER/TEACHER/GRANDMOTHER

gatekeeper press

Columbus, Ohio

Top Students, Top Parents: Good Students Begin at Home
2nd Edition

Published by Gatekeeper Press
2167 Stringtown Rd, Suite 109
Columbus, OH 43123-2989
www.GatekeeperPress.com

Notice: All recommendations and suggestions are made without any guarantees on the part of the author. Success or failure incurred by following recommended suggestions and advice is determined strictly by the parent or caregivers of the child.

Publisher's Cataloging-in-Publication Data

Names: Burns, Kathleen, author.
Title: Top students , top parents : good students begin at home, 2nd edition / Kathleen Burns.
Description: Includes bibliographical references. | Columbus, OH: Gatekeeper Press, 2021.
Identifiers: LCCN: 2020945545 | ISBN: 9781662904455 (pbk.) | 9781662904462 (ebook)
Subjects: LCSH Parenting. | Early childhood education--Parent participation--Handbooks, manuals, etc. | Education, Elementary--Parent participation--Handbooks, manuals, etc. | Language arts--Handbooks, manuals, etc. | Reading (Early childhood) | Parent and child--Handbooks, manuals, etc. | BISAC FAMILY & RELATIONSHIPS / Education | FAMILY & RELATIONSHIPS / Parenting / General
Classification: LCC LB1139.35.P37 B87 2021 | DDC 372.13/0281--dc23

Dedicated to My Kids,

With Love

ACKNOWLEDGEMENTS

Many people contributed to the creation of this book:

First, my children, Sue, Nick and Paul, of whom I am extremely proud and to whom I will forever be indebted. They were my first and foremost teachers. Together, we loved and learned, overcoming and benefiting from obstacles that, fortunately, many families will never know. It was through our experiences of living through the trials, tribulations, and heartache of serious and extended physical illness in someone we dearly loved, that we were able to develop a deep understanding of each other and ourselves, as well as a rich and rewarding empathy toward other parents and their children.

I would also like to recognize all the students whom I taught for the twenty years that I was a teacher, as well as their parents. They taught me more than they will ever know. It was the parents who came to me repeatedly and asked, "How can I help my child?" and their children who cried out silently and helplessly for understanding and guidance that gave me the persistence to make this book a reality.

Finally, I would like to show appreciation to all the scientists, doctors, psychologists, neuropsychologists, principals, teachers and authors in the bibliography, whose writings and research contributed to the ideas, suggestions and advice contained in this book. May our mutual mission be fulfilled.

AUTHOR'S COMMENTS

Most children are born with the potential to become a top student and eventually successful adults. However, the parents and home environment determine the child's opportunity to pursue this success. Too many parents are not doing their job. They believe that school is the beginning of the child's education. In reality, Kindergarten is six years too late. According to scientific research, the critical learning period for children is between the ages of 8 and 18 months, and by the time they are 8 years old they are already set in molds that determine their academic futures. While preschool programs beginning as early as age 3 certainly help, the child's critical learning period is still missed.

School can be equated to a jungle, where the law is "survival of the fittest." When we send our children to kindergarten, they automatically fall into the top, middle, or bottom of the class. Those whose parents give them the best foundation for learning during their preschool years are the fittest. They begin school with a head start; they're confident, have the beginning of a healthy self-esteem, have advanced vocabularies, speak in complete sentences, and learn their ABC's and numbers with ease. Having done a good job preparing them for school, their parents help and support them by making certain they understand their assignments and do their homework. They provide them with an educationally rich home environment, read to them, restrict their TV and games, and plan activities away from home that will contribute to their educational repertoire. These lucky children become the elite of their class. Year after year they receive the best grades and all the honors, and awards. From high school they go on to college, and from there, they work their way into top paying jobs and the upper echelons of society.

At the other end of the spectrum are the children who receive little preparation for school. Rather than bedtime stories, their days usually end in front of the television. When they enter school, they're already at the bottom of the class; they're shy and withdrawn, have poor language development and comprehension skills, must learn how to follow simple instructions, and have difficulty learning their ABCs and numbers. They can't compete, because the top students are learning much more rapidly, becoming further ahead, while these poor kids struggle to learn what the others already know when they enter school. Many of them never catch up, because they don't do their work, or even understand how to do it. They eventually give up, because no matter how hard they try, they're always behind, never understand, and most always fail. Dropping out of high school is the easy way out for them, but makes them prime targets for gangs, drugs, and crime, destined to work at menial paying jobs, or to be on welfare the rest of their lives.

Why is there such a discrepancy in the manner in which children are prepared for school? The difference is, parents of the top students know how to prepare and support their children, and they are willing to go the extra mile to see that their children receive the best start in life.

For decades, American students have been underperforming compared to other nations. Billions of dollars continue to be thrown away on the same old remedies in hopes of increasing students' test scores: better teachers, new books, updated curriculum, and expensive studies to determine how to help kids learn. None of these "fix-its" have worked.

It's time we put our efforts in the right place…the parents and the home environment. There will be some parents who can't do better for a number of reasons beyond their control, but there would be plenty who would be grateful to learn ways they can help their children get a better start in life. This book is for the parents who are able and willing to go the extra mile in order to help their children become all they can be.

Preface

My purpose for writing this book is to **teach parents how to prepare their children for successful learning in school and how to support them when they get there.**

For the sake of simplicity throughout the book, I address either "*parents*" or the "*mother.*" I have no intention of leaving the father out, but studies suggest that the most influential person in the child's life is the mother, because she bears the child and spends the most time raising it. **Fathers are extremely important to the child's development and when possible, are encouraged to follow the same suggestions and advice as the mothers.**

The parents needn't have an educational background in order to follow my suggestions, but those who already have children may need to adjust their lifestyle in order to accommodate some of them. For those who will soon have a baby or already have preschool children, they can begin anew to make their home and relationship with their children conducive to their learning. The suggestions take into consideration the parents' busy day-to-day schedule, whether the mother home-schools her children, is a work-at-home mom, or one who works away from home. The advice and suggestions are directed toward parents with children from infancy up to about age twelve or older. The book is divided into three parts:

Part I   Infancy and Up
Part II   Reading and Writing
Part III   School Success

Natural Opportunities

The main premise of this book is not to make children geniuses, or to send them to school at the head of the class, but rather *to help parents prepare them for school and future success,* **simply by the way they talk to them and by making learning experiences out of everyday activities in which their families already participate. Most of the ideas are presented via simple, hands-on advice that can be utilized any time the parents have contact with their children: during meals, while cleaning house, working in the garden, sitting in the dentist's office, bathing, or during recreation. Par** *ents will learn to identify educational opportunities and teachable moments, and if there aren't any, they learn how to make them up so that teaching their children will become second nature.*

Being so very aware of the daily responsibilities and time constraints mothers face, I am careful not to suggest they spend sit-down time teaching their children, with minor exceptions. For the same reason, it is not my intention to make parents feel that they must follow all suggestions. *Mothers should feel free to go through the suggestions and select the ones that appeal to them and their children, and ignore those they can't fit into their schedules.*

Fun and Games

Most of the activities for *preschool and early grade children* are based upon having fun while learning, as well as taking advantage of their natural curiosity. In any situation involving teaching very young children, whether it's how to get them to pick up their toys, to eat their vegetables or to learn educational concepts, *fun is the key. Learning to do things because they must be done is a gradual process that children acquire with maturity.* What appeals to very young children is whether an activity is enjoyable or not. If it's fun, then you have their attention and cooperation. If not, then it will take a battle to get them to do it. *Parents and teachers who are aware of this principle are far ahead in the game of teaching and how young children learn.*

Too Much, Too Soon

It is impossible to over-emphasize the importance of letting preschool children learn naturally. This would be indicated by questions the children ask, or through situations the parents create in the course of *their normal daily contact*. Preschool children cannot be pressured to learn, especially when they're not ready to understand the concept. Children will learn when ready, never before. But *most often* they learn *when their curiosity is aroused. No amount of fun and games can entice them to cooperate if they are not ready*.

Formal Teaching

Formal teaching is any organized teaching that is not instigated or encouraged by the child. It may include drills, flash cards, and teaching materials that require the child to sit and pay attention. Formal teaching should be introduced in school around age five when the child should be ready to begin to learn to sit still, pay attention, and con centrate on what is being taught. Before that time, any attempt at formal teaching may result in dismal failure, stress, and educational burnout. Formal teaching is best left for the teachers when the child is in school, or for home-school parents at age appropriate levels.

Most Important Suggestions for All Parents!

The magnitude of the suggestions and activities in this book would appear to be overwhelming to the working mother and even the stay-at-home moms; however, ***if mothers do the best they can to teach their children through daily verbal contact, provide good behavior the children can model, and read to them daily, they will greatly enhance their children's learning years***. All of these skills are available in this book for the parents to learn.

TABLE OF CONTENTS

PART I

 LAYING THE FOUNDATION FOR SUCCESS
INFANCY AND ABOVE

Chapter 1

LISTEN TO THE EXPERTS

Harvard

Cambridge University

Washington University

Duke   University

University of Alaska

Baylor College

Kansas University

University of Alaska

Columbia University

Stanford

Wayne State

University of Konstanz

New York State

University of Illinois

"Education is not preparation for life;
education is life itself."

John Dewey

This chapter contains summaries and conclusions of several research projects conducted by child development specialists. Each project is accompanied by the authors' names and the titles of their reports. Many recommendations in this book are based on the results of these studies. It is very important that the parents read this chapter in its entirety, two or three times if necessary, in order to fully understand the importance of their role in their children's education and future success.

At one time it was the general consensus that intelligence was innate, that children's mentality was predestined at birth, and that their environmental nurturing had minor effects on the type of people they turned out to be. According to the studies referenced in this chapter, this is far from the truth.

MOST SIGNIFICANT CONCLUSIONS

- It has been established that genes may form the basis for intelligence; however, high quality childcare, early education, and social contacts provide a lasting impact on the child's intelligence and ability to learn. A child born with high learning potential will lose it without the necessary stimulation of positive experiences and favorable environmental factors. If preschool children are not prepared for school learning, none of our strategies for teaching them will be as effective when they begin school.

- The critical learning period is between the ages of eight and eighteen months. Although an outstanding quality of the brain is its ability to change, by the time children are eight years old the basis for their academic future is set. The older the child becomes, the more difficult it is to help him overcome the lack of proper education and stimulation during his preschool years. If parents don't provide the necessary experiences during these crucial years, the best that educators can do is to prepare the children for unskilled jobs.

- The amount of language spoken directly to the child during her first three years is critical to her intellectual development and ability to learn. Conversation, in the form of lengthy explanations, feedback, approval, and questions parents ask their child will significantly increase her I.Q. How much language the child hears during the preschool years determines how intelligent she will become.

- Satisfaction of the child's natural curiosity about objects and sounds in his immediate environment is mandatory for his intellectual development. The curiosity of children raised in restricted environments decreases with age and se-

- limits their ability to build upon knowledge gained from satisfaction of their curiosity; whereas babies and preschool children who are allowed to explore their surroundings, encouraged to investigate objects and sounds, and given various playthings have an increasing desire to learn as they become older.

Regardless of parents' education, children raised in homes where there are 500 books attain 3.2 years further education after high school, compared to those raised in homes without books.

Harvard Preschool Project
Conducted by Burton L. White, Ph.D.
13 years research with 17 full-time researchers and over 100 families.

Dr. Burton L. White, Ph.D., 1929-2013, devoted much of his entire life to studying the development of the human being. In 1965 he became director of the Harvard Preschool Project, the most intensive research program ever performed on the development of children within their own families during their first years of life. He was founder and director of the Center for Parent Education in Newton, Massachusetts, and the senior consultant to Missouri's New Parents as Teachers project. He taught at Harvard University, Brandeis University, and Tufts University. He wrote numerous books, the most noteworthy of which was, The *Origins of Human Competence,* with co-authors Barbara T. Kaban and Jane S. Attanucci, and *Educating the Infant and Toddler.* In all, Dr. White spent years exploring how adults become the way they are and how to help all children achieve their full potential.

Following are the findings of thirteen years of research which Dr. White directed with the help of seventeen full-time researchers and the cooperation of over a hundred families:

Importance of Age

- The critical period of the origins of human competence was determined to be between the ages of eight and eighteen months, during which time the child's experiences do more to influence his future intellectual competence than at any time before or after.

Language

- By far, the most effective type of educational experience contributing to a child's intelligence was live language directly heard by the eleven-to thirty-six month infant. This was not to include television, radio or overheard conversations.

- Language spoken to the child related to her current interest or as a result of her inquiries plays a key role in language development and fluency.

Curiosity and Education

- Curiosity is intimately related to education. Restriction of crawling and touching objects in the surrounding environment had negative effects on motor control and was detrimental to the child's intellectual development. This occurred when parents confined their child for long periods of time to playpens, jump seats, cribs, or other restrictive devices. These children became bored because they could not satisfy their curiosity or practice newly developing motor skills.

- The ability to explore their surroundings and receiving the encouragement to investigate objects and sounds in the infant and toddler stages seemed to lead to much higher levels of desire for learning and satisfaction of curiosity in the older child.

Good Parents

- provided stimulating environments, complete with colorful objects and items to manipulate in order to arouse the child's curiosity.
- made themselves available to support and give explanations related to the child's curiosity.
- set limits and gave firm, consistent discipline when necessary, accompanied by deep love and respect.

Family Environment and Major Role Models

- The most dominant environmental factor in the life of the child is her mother. She influences her child's experiences more than any other person or circumstances.

- In the case of the mother working, the child should be placed in the care of people who have the greatest love for her, preferably the grandparents or other close relatives.

Meaningful Differences in
the Everyday Experience of Young American Children
By Betty Hart and Todd Risley

Betty Hart, 1927-2012 was Professor Emeritus of Human Development at the University of Kansas, and was also Senior Scientist at the Schiefelbusch Institute for Life Span Studies at the University of Kansas. Todd Risley, 1937-2007 was Professor of Psychology at the University of Alaska, and Senior Scientist at the Schiefelbusch Institute for Life Span Studies at The University of Kansas. Doctors Hart and Risley both began their careers in the early 1960's at the Institute for Child Development at the University of Washington. They cooperatively introduced the basic procedures of *adult attention* and *time-out,* now routinely taught and used in teaching and parenting. They also introduced the procedures for *shaping speech* and *language,* widely used in special education. In 1965 they began thirty years of collaborative work at The University of Kansas, where they established preschool intervention programs in poverty-stricken neighborhoods in Kansas City. Their study of what children actually do and say in day-care and preschool, and their publications on *incidental teaching,* form the empirical base for contemporary child-centered teaching practices in preschool and special education.

Findings

This study was based on the comparison of the vocabulary development of poor school children with that of children whose parents were university professors. For two years, a child between the ages of seven and twelve months and his parent, usually the mother, were observed once a month in the homes of forty-two families. The observer tape-recorded everything said between the parent and child, and took notes about what happened. *The observations continued until the children were three years old, during which time the welfare parents spoke an average of 600 words per hour to their children, working-class parents spoke 1,200 words, and professionals spoke 2,000 words.*

Language

- Parents' race, economic status and education had no effect on the children's language and I.Q. tests. Those children whose parents talked a lot, gave much feedback and approval, offered lengthy explanations and asked questions, scored higher on an I.Q. test and on measures of vocabulary development at age three.

- When tested again in the third grade, their scores continued to indicate the influence of the early pattern of parental behavior.

- Children achieving the highest level were those spoken to four times more an hour than those scoring the lowest. The conclusion was that even poor, un-educated parents are capable of providing the kinds of experiences required for healthy intellectual development; however, if they aren't taught how to provide these experiences in the home, the best that educators can hope to do for their children is prepare them for unskilled jobs. And if the parents do not provide these experiences, making up for the deficiency with remedial programs after the age of four or in school is practically impossible.

- Parents' race, economic status, and education were irrelevant; what really mat-tered is what parents did. Those children whose parents talked a lot, giving much feedback and approval, lengthy explanations, and asked questions scored higher on an I.Q. test and on measures of vocabulary development at age three. When the same children were tested again in vocabulary and I.Q. in the third grade, their scores continued to indicate the influence of these early patterns of parental behavior

Feedback

- Professional parents more often commented positively on their children's be-havior such as, "You're doing a good job," or "Good."
- Low-income parents were far more likely to criticize than to praise and used more negative words such as "no," "don't," "stop," and "quit."

Remedial Measures

- If remedial measures were taken to bring the welfare children's language experi-ences up to par with children of working class parents, they would need to hear 63,000 additional words, and 1,100 positive comments per week, totaling forty hours per week of supplemental care from birth onward. This was relatively impossible from a practical standpoint.

- It would take generations of gradual improvements in families in order to over-come the past negative practices passed down from parents. It is recommended that parents as well as mentors and parental aides, be taught good child-rearing practices to be imitated by their children when they are parents.

Rethinking the Brain: New Insights into Early Development
Families and Work Institute, New York, NY, 1997, Rima Shore

This report was inspired by the *I Am Your Child* campaign, a national public awareness campaign whose purpose is to make the public aware of the important ways a child's brain develops during the first three years of life, and to make early childhood development a priority for our nation. Founders of the campaign are Rob Reiner and Michele Singer Reiner, Ellen Gilbert of International Creative Management, and a broad range of experts from the early childhood fields.

Findings

- Although human development and learning depends upon a critical overlapping of the person's genes, the quality of the preschool child's environment and social experience, nutrition, environment, care, stimulation, and teachings all have a decisive, long-lasting impact on the child's well-being and ability to learn.

- The capacity of a child's brain expands more between birth and age three than at any other time. Affectionate, responsive care by the child's caregiver seems to be a major ingredient for protecting the child to some degree against future effects of stress or trauma, as well as contributing to a curious, confident, and capable learner.

- An outstanding quality of the brain is its ability to change, but timing is of critical importance. The human brain is not fixed at birth… it can be helped to overcome shortcomings, inexperience, or to improve development, but the intervention must be within a specified time period.

- High quality childcare and early education can increase children's opportunity for later success in school; however, most American preschool children who are in day care are in facilities of poor to mediocre quality.

- Educators report that thirty-five percent of American kindergarten children arrive at school unprepared to respond to the instruction and interactions they encounter in their classrooms. Only fifty percent of infants and toddlers are read to consistently by their parents.

- By the time children are eight years old, they are already set in molds that deter

- mine their academic futures, whether it be of success or failure. Researchers are able to predict students' dropout potential based on their school performance and social relationships in the third grade, some even based on the quality of care and support they received in the first years of life.

**500 Books in the Home, "Family Scholarly Culture
and Educational Success: Books and schooling in 27 Nations"**
Conducted by Mariah Evans of the University of Nevada, and four researchers in the U. S. and Australia, published in the journal, *Research in Social Stratification and Mobility,* 2010, based on data from 73,249 people

---

Relevance of the findings of this study to American children's future: According to the U.S. Census Bureau's *American Community Survey*, students who have some college or an associate's degree, but not a bachelor's degree, earn an average of $7,213 more annually than those with just a high school education. Those who attain a bachelor's degree earn $21,185 more each year, on average, than those with just high school diplomas. Having books in the home can dramatically increase children's level of education, leading to significantly higher paying jobs in their future.

Findings

- Regardless of parent's education, whether illiterate or university educated, children raised in homes where there are 500 books, attain 3.2 years further education compared to those raised in bookless homes.

- Even children of illiterate parents in China who had home libraries of 500 books showed an astounding 6.6 more years of schooling than Chinese children without books in their home. Results show that having books in the home has a greater impact on children raised in the least educated families.

- Even having as few as 20 books in the home carries an impressive impact, resulting in a higher education level as having no books, while increasing the number of books adds even more to the educational benefit.

- Having books in the home had a stronger effect on the children's education than the education of both of the parents, the country's GDP, the country's political system, or the father's occupation.

- The most impressive results of the study were that having books in the home had a greater impact on children from the least educated families than those where parents had college educations.

Chapter 2

DANGERS OF ELECTRONIC
ENTERTAINMENT

"So PLEASE, oh PLEASE, WE BEG, WE PRAY, Go throw your TV set away,
And in its place you can install, A lovely bookshelf on the wall."

Roald Dahl, Charlie and the Chocolate Factory

Television and computers are robbing children of the benefits they used to get through physical activity. Years ago, kids had nothing else to do except play and do chores; they played hard, riding bikes, running, climbing, digging, playing with the hose, building things…whether indoors or out, they moved all the time. Never did you see a child just sitting or lying down doing nothing, except when they were sleeping. ***Today, twenty to thirty years later, most kids don't play outside anymore, nor inside either; the only place we see them is sitting and lying down all the time, watching television or using their smartphones.***

Their world has changed drastically. There's no time left for play; they're too busy with other, more advanced, fun things to do like television, computer games, the Internet, tablets, and smartphones. ***Parents love this modern technology. They're the greatest babysitters, and the parents don't even have to pay them. The kids don't fight or make any noise; they don't make any messes, and parents don't have to worry about them getting into trouble.*** Kids sit passively for hours, eyes glued on the screens, not a peep out of them, while parents get their stuff done in peace and quiet.

This is not to say that all media viewing is bad. There are many programs available that are educational and fun to watch for children, from preschool through elementary age, that encourage brain development and increase children's learning skills such as language, vocabulary, practice with letters, phonics and counting; however parents need to select the programs and spend time viewing them with their children so they can teach them. They need to talk to their children about what they see on television and *set parental controls* so children can't watch forbidden programs. There are numerous excellent websites that will help you select appropriate programs and how to monitor your children's viewing. Check out the following:

What screen time and screen media do to your child's brain.
Television and children: University of Michigan
9 amazing TV shows developed by common sense media
Toddlers, preschool, TV, computer by Aha Parenting
Television, commercials and your child

Research

Research indicates 3-to 4-year-olds spend 14 hours a week watching television and 8 hours online; 5-to 15-year-olds spend 13 hours a week watching television and 15 hours online. Then add more hours that they spend on their smartphones each day.

What time is left for learning, growing, and communicating? Its further reported that 75 percent of children have television sets in their bedrooms, and 50 percent of North American homes have television on all day and well into the night.

The American Academy of Pediatrics (APP) recommends no screen time for babies and toddlers, one hour a day for preschool children, and two hours a day for older children. *I do not recommend any television at all on school nights; they're hectic enough with dinner, homework, bathing, and getting school things ready for the next day. Two hours of television (or even an hour) would ruin homework time, school preparation or family time, and there would not be enough time left for a bedtime story before lights out. Television for school-aged children should be limited to two hours on weekends and summer months, and then it should be severely monitored by the parents.*

What's really sad is that many parents don't realize the danger involved in excessive use of this media. When children have their eyes glued to the screen for hours, their minds and bodies shut down. They don't move or think and don't even hear someone talking to them. Doctors fear that due to under-development of their brains and bodies, this generation may have a shorter life span than their parents.

Negative Conclusions

A simple search of the Internet will give you an eyeful of conclusions of studies reached by doctors and scientists in Canada, Hong Kong, England, Japan, Australia, the U.S., and elsewhere around the world about the dangers our children are subject to when they watch excessive television and other electronic devices. Following are some of these shocking conclusions of the harmful effects excessive electronic media causes:

Preschool Children

- hinders creativity and imagination
- alters brain structure
- causes developmental delays
- promotes coordination disorders
- retards good balance
- restricts communication skills
- affects development of good reading skills

School Children

- contributes to obesity
- prevents social and family interaction
- discourages creativity and art activities
- prevents healthy play activities
- allows negative role models
- gives children a false sense of the world
- competes with homework and reading time
- inhibits coordination development
- promotes behavior disorders
- leads to reading disabilities
- hinders concentration and memory
- causes poor overall school achievement
- promotes self-discipline problems
- causes attention disorders
- encourages aggressive behavior

Health Issues

- higher cholesterol in later years
- lower cardiovascular fitness
- more frequent ADHD
- potential autism
- obesity and diabetes
- retarded physical development
- unhealthy adult life styles
- narrow arteries in the eyes
- higher risk of high blood pressure

Psychological Problems

- loneliness
- depression
- withdrawal
- anxiety
- poor self-esteem
- Internet addiction

- Smart phone addiction
- sleep disorders

Unacceptable Behavior

- shows aggressive behavior positively
- exposes children to violence
- overabundance of violence, alcohol, drugs and sex
- popular actors engage in speed driving
- causes confusion over right and wrong behavior

Materialism and Low Self-Esteem

- emphasizes importance of expensive clothes
- popularity associated with beauty and clothes
- content causes dissatisfaction with body image
- overemphasis on athletic abilities

Chapter 3

. . . .

INFANCY/PRESCHOOL
LANGUAGE DEVELOPMENT

"My love of reading and the English language is something given to me by my parents and I've passed it on to my children."

Corin Tucker 1973 (Singer/Guitarist)

If you just browsed through Chapter One, *"Listen to the Experts,"* I encourage you to go back and read it again. It contains the summaries of studies conducted on why children's language development in professional families is so advanced, compared to those in middle class and welfare families. *According to these studies, children achieving the highest level of development by age three, and again in third grade, were spoken to four times more an hour than those scoring the lowest. <u>By the time they were three years old the children of the professional parents heard 2,000 words per hour compared to 1,200 words from working-class parents and 600 words from welfare parents.</u> The conclusion is that even poor, uneducated parents are capable of providing the kinds of experiences required for healthy intellectual development; however, if they aren't taught how to provide these experiences in the home, the best that educators can hope to do for their children is to prepare them for unskilled jobs.*

How unbelievably simple! *According to these studies, just by talking to your babies and preschool children, you can considerably increase their intelligence and ability to learn. These studies even indicate that the children of talkative parents are better readers and have much larger vocabularies than their peers by third grade. But there are a few conditions:*

1. You can't just set the child in front of the TV, or let her listen to you talk on the phone.
2. There must be a lot of language, and it must be spoken directly to the child.
3. The language you use must be of good quality.

Speak Proper English

The best way to teach your child good language skills is to use them yourself. It's important that you use good grammar so you can teach your child how to speak properly as he learns to talk. *Keep in mind that he will speak the way you do.* If you have a good grasp of English grammar, you will pass it on to your child when you speak to him. *Adults who use words and phrases like, "me and him," "I don't got," "I ain't," or "I seen," are hampered considerably in the job market and their social relationships.* If your child already has poor speaking habits, then correct him kindly, but relentlessly, until he begins to speak properly. If you have a problem speaking properly, even if you cannot change yourself, at least try to become aware of the proper way to speak so you can teach your child. Then challenge him to correct you, as well. Make it fun by deliberately using improper English to see if he catches you.

When your child goes to school and associates with other children, he will pick up the poor grammar they use, even if you don't use it yourself. Be on your guard so it doesn't become deep-seated and more difficult to correct. Keep your corrections positive. No one likes to be corrected when it's done in a humiliating manner. When you hear him speaking the wrong way and you correct him, praise his efforts when he rephrases and shows an effort to speak properly. Help your child recognize poor grammar by deliberately using it in front of him, so he may correct you. Make a game of it. When he can substitute the proper usage, you will know he's learning. Some of the most common grammatical mistakes and their corrections are:

Incorrect	Correct
Me and him are going to the ball game.	*He and I are going to the ball game.*
Him and I are going to the ball game.	*He and I are going to the ball game.*
John and me are going to the ball game.	*John and I are going to the ball game.*
I ain't got a pencil.	*I don't have a pencil.*
I don't got a pencil.	*I don't have a pencil.*
He gots my pencil.	*He has my pencil.*
He ain't going to the ball game.	*He isn't going to the ball game.*
Can I go to the ball game?	*May I go to the ball game?*
I seen a bear.	*I saw a bear.*
You do good in Math.	*You do well in Math.*
You paint very good.	*You paint very well.*
He paints nice.	*He paints nicely.*
Joey is going with John and I.	*Joey is going with John and me.*
Joey is going with me and John.	*Joey is going with John and me.*

Please! No Baby Talk.

As long as you're going to be concentrating on talking to your child, be mindful of baby talk. Some babies and young children who are encouraged to speak baby talk in their formative years may have difficulty learning to distinguish between some sounds when they are older. Typical baby talk substitutes the sound of w for l. For example, words like little, love, lollypop, and laugh are pronounced wittle, wove, waweypop and waugh.

When babies hear and speak the w sound for the l sound the first three to four years of their life, they have difficulty finally mastering the l sound when they're older. This may not only cause a school-age child considerable embarrassment, but also makes reading difficult for her. **There's nothing wrong with baby talk at the appropriate time; however, in order to prevent it from becoming a problem, parents must help their child overcome it gradually, as he matures, by always speaking distinctly and using clear and precise pronunciation.** If the child says, "I wove you," say, "Mommy loves you, too." Have fun with him by showing him how to say "la la la la" and exaggerate the movement of the tongue. If the child is school-age and shows no improvement while trying to help him develop correct pronunciations, ask her pediatrician if she thinks it's a problem and would recommend speech therapy, or perhaps the school will recommend therapy.

Two thousand words per hour sounds overwhelming, but don't be intimidated. *It turns out to be only about 15 minutes of talking during the child's awake hours.* Once you learn what you can talk about, you will see how easy it is to reach that goal without even planning or thinking about what you are going to say. And you'll probably end up talking a lot more than just fifteen minutes. You needn't be concerned about how much you talk until the child is about eight months old. Just follow my suggestions and you will speak more than enough words, and you won't even have to count them.

Keep Talking

Parents begin bonding with their child the day the baby is born by holding, touching, humming, talking and singing. Babies love to hear *parentese,* which is a lot of fun for parents, too. This is when you exaggerate the vowels and stretch them out in a high pitched, sing-song voice, so that when saying the words, "hello baby," they sound like "helooooo baybeeeee."

If you don't already have one, I highly recommend a baby carrier or a sling; one in which you can hold the infant against your chest facing you as an infant, and facing away from you when she's old enough to be interested in things around her. She will watch what you're doing or where you are going. When my children were babies, we didn't have baby carriers, so as soon as they were old enough to sit up, I would prop them up with pillows and rolled up towels in their high chair and set them in the kitchen so I could talk to them, and they could see me and hear me make noises.

Something else that you can do is use the car seat as a carrier which you can set any where in the house, so the baby can be with you whenever she's awake. But neither of these are as effective as the sling. While carrying the baby in a sling, she can be a part of everything you do, whether its mixing and measuring, making a salad, washing dishes, or shopping. She'll watch and listen as you tell her what you are doing. Use short sentences and lots of different words. Here are just a few of the everyday activities that you can talk to her about:

- Setting the table
- Washing vegetables
- Making a salad
- Working in the garden
- Getting groceries
- Putting groceries away
- Watering the garden
- Going outside to get the mail
- Baking cookies
- Putting on your makeup
- Combing your hair

Some examples of what to say:

While getting ready for dinner: *"Let's set the table for dinner. First we put ice cubes in the glasses; then fill them with water. Cold water is nice to have with dinner. Here, let me put some water on your hand. Do you feel the water? Water is good for you. Pretty soon Suzie will be drinking water from a glass, just like Mommy and Daddy. Next we put the silverware on the table. Here's the fork. It goes on the left side of the plate. The knife and spoon go on the right side of the plate, and the napkin goes underneath them. Let's see now, what else do we need? I know…salt and pepper, and we need ketchup and butter, too."*

While getting ready to go shopping:
"Mommy and Suzie are going shopping. We need to buy some bread and milk for supper tonight, but first we have to change your diaper. There, now you're dry. Do you feel better now? Let's get ready to go. It's cold outside! Let's put on your snowsuit. I know you don't like it, sweetie, but you'll be nice and warm. First let's put your arms in. There! Now for your legs. There we go. That wasn't so bad, was it? Here goes the zipper, zip, zip, zip! Hurray! Suzie is all ready to go. Now Mommy is going to put her coat on. Oh,

where are my keys? We can't go shopping without the car. Here they are, right on the cabinet. Okay, we're on our way!"

While looking out the window:

"Look at the little squirrel on the grass! See his big tail? It looks like he's shaking it at us. I think he wants something to eat. Oh look! He's running away. See him climb the tree? That must be where he lives."

"I see trees and grass and, oh, there's a little girl playing on the grass. And look, there's a puppy! He must belong to the little girl. See how his tail is wagging? What is the little girl doing? She's playing jump rope with her friend. Look at all the cars passing by. There goes a red one. Look! Here comes another one. That was a lady driving."

While putting groceries away:

"Let's put the groceries away. Mommy's going to put all the canned food here on the cabinet. Here's green beans...mmm. Suzie likes green beans; here's canned tomatoes and look here! Your baby food, peaches! Baby likes peaches. And what else does Suzie like? Applesauce is your favorite. And here's bananas. Yummy! Now where do I put these? Right here in the cabinet on the shelf with all the other canned stuff. Here's milk and butter and cheese. These all go in the refrigerator and hamburger and ice cream go in the freezer. Suzie really likes ice cream? You may have some after you eat your dinner. Now where would the Kleenex and bathroom tissue go? That's right, here in the bathroom closet."

While walking around the room:

Point at different objects and talk about them, such as, *"Look at the picture on the wall. See the buildings? Which one is taller? And here's a big lake next to the buildings. See the boat in the water? Look, Suzie. This is Mommy's plant hanging from the ceiling. See its leaves? They're green and shiny. Here, touch one. Can you say pretty?"*

These examples may sound silly in writing, but when actually speaking you would use different words and emphasis that will interest your baby and cause her to listen more intently. You might even use some "parenteese."

Repetition

Babies must not only hear a lot of language, but words need to be repeated in order for them to become part of their comprehension vocabulary. So don't be concerned about showing and talking about the same things too often...it's repetition of the names of objects that causes babies to build their unspoken vocabularies that they will soon be able to verbalize. When the baby hears the word, *bottle*, for example, over and over again… "Do you want your *bottle*? "Mommy's warming your *bottle*." "Daddy's going to give you your *bottle*," the baby's going to associate the word bottle with the actual bottle and will know what "bottle" means when he wants it and hears its name.

If he points to his toy bunny and Momma says, "Do you want your bunny? Say bunny. Ask Mamma to give you your bunny," he will learn how the bunny's name sounds, and when he tries to say its name and Momma claps her hands and says, "Yes, Bunny," he will learn the bunny's name and will soon speak it. In this way, the more often the baby hears the names of things he relates to, the more his vocabulary will expand.

Nursery Rhymes

Rhyming poems and stories have a special appeal to babies and preschoolers. One of the most pleasurable times both you and your child will have is while reading *Mother Goose Rhymes*. I still remember my little girl singing "I'm a Little Teapot," while bending over and using her arms for the spout and handle. When would a preschooler learn words like teapot and spout if she didn't learn them when mother reads to her? Parents can capitalize on children's enthusiasm and enjoyment of rhymes by initiating activities that will build a larger vocabulary, while bringing them closer to actual reading. Being able to recite a few nursery rhymes is encouraged for kindergarten qualifications in some schools.

Curiosity

Again, see Chapter One for the following conclusions:

"Satisfaction of the child's natural curiosity of objects and sounds in her immediate environment is mandatory for her intellectual development. Crawling infants and preschool children who are allowed to explore their surroundings, encouraged to investigate objects and sounds, and given various playthings have an increasing desire for learning as they became older."

Babies are born naturally curious and interested in everything around them. To keep their minds developing, parents have to supply them with a multitude of objects that make noise and music, things to see and feel, and continuous new experiences. As they grow, their curiosity expands…the more they can see and do, the more their brain develops and more intelligent they will become. Many of the activities that mother performs and talks about to her baby when she is carrying her in the sling contribute to expansion of her curiosity.

Imagine a baby confined to a playpen or her bed for hours, bored with the same objects that she sees every day, nothing new, same rattles and colors. Compare this child with one who is supplied with colorful scarves and objects, toys that she can shake or that rattle, bells and music to hear, things to pick up and throw, and lots of language and singing.

When my kids were babies I used to have a box in which to save things I came upon that would be neat play things. These included such items as: plastic food containers, empty milk and juice bottles, empty thread spools, vitamin bottles, lids from jars of all kinds, large plastic soup spoons and ladles, measuring spoons, and cups...anything that they could throw, roll, bang with, or bounce around that were safe. My babies' favorite place to play was in the lower part of my cabinets that held my cooking pans and lids. The pleasure they got from playing with these was more than worth the time it took to wash them before putting food in them.

A word of caution about small objects – make certain you don't give babies things small enough to swallow or poke their eyes or throats with. Anything with long, thin handles such as spoons, butter knives, forks, pencils, or objects they can swallow like coins, rings, rocks, beads, bottle caps are all dangerous to babies.

Sparking Curiosity

As your children grow, their vocabularies increase at an amazingly rapid rate. ***Remember, babies from eight months to thirty-six months learn faster, and more, than at any other time in their lives.*** Your communication should graduate from talking *to* them to talking *with* them. Arouse their curiosity by asking them questions and encouraging them to ask you about things. Provide positive feedback to their questions and behavior. When the toddler brings you things, it means she is curious and wants to know about it. If she points to a little bug crawling on the floor, stop what you're doing and observe it with her, and tell her what it is. When she begins to ask you questions, never ignore them, or tell her you're too busy. Even if she's not talking yet, you can arouse her interest just by showing her things and letting her touch them, such as a simple hair brush while you brush her hair, or show her how you brush your hair. Let her touch the bristles, then put the brush in her hand and help her brush her hair. Following are several ways you can promote curiosity in your child:

- Ask thought-provoking questions that make her think instead of just making statements. For example, "Oh, look at the worms! Why do you think they're stretched out on the sidewalk? Perhaps they're cold and the sidewalk is warm. I wonder where they're going?" Or, "Look at the beautiful butterfly! I wonder why it's sitting on the flower. Is it eating the flower? Maybe it likes the fragrance of the flower." Explain what fragrance means. Let her smell the flower. Observe the butterfly flapping its wings and how it keeps flying to other flowers. Tell her the butterfly is eating nectar, something sweet inside the flower.

- Spend time with him in the yard with a magnifying glass looking up close at so many things: textures of tree trunks, blades of grass, grains of sand, insects, the insides of flowers, and how worms look real close.

- Ask questions such as, "I wonder why birds are afraid of us?" "I wonder why the clock stopped ticking?" "I wonder why spiders like to come inside." "I wonder why squirrels run away from us?"

- Avoid asking questions that require plain yes and no answers, such as, "What do you like to do at the park," as opposed to, "Do you like to go to the park?" Help him answer questions in complete sentences, such as "I like to go to the park, because I get to feed the ducks." rather than saying, " Feed the ducks."

- Encourage your child to discuss what happens soon after an event occurs such as relating what she did at the park soon after Daddy brings her home, what she just ate for breakfast, the places Grandma took her to shop, why her shoes are wet, and how Chip behaved when she and Daddy took him to the veterinarian.

Singing

Babies love singing, whether it's *Rock-a-Bye Baby, You Are My Sunshine,* "The Wheels on the Bus Go Round and Round," or songs you make up. Instead of saying the words when you talk to him, sing them. One thing nice about singing to your baby is that he doesn't care if you're off-key or don't have a nice voice. Before you know it, he'll be singing the songs, too. Play CD's with baby songs and different sorts of music…soft, rhythmic, and marching. When you sing, baby learns more words and will soon begin to speak what he hears. It all counts as hearing language.

As I mentioned earlier, there are so many ways you can speak to your child that once you become aware of them you won't even have to count them, and before you know it, you may be speaking far more than the recommended number. ***Remember, the baby's first eight-to thirty-six months are crucial for mental development, and the more language he hears, the higher his IQ and the more successful he will become in later life.***

Chapter 4

THE BODY-BRAIN CONNECTION

"For a small child there is no division between playing and learning, between the things he or she does 'just for fun' and things that are 'educational.' The child learns while living, and any part of living that is enjoyable is also play."

Penelope Leach

Coordination

Gross motor coordination leads to strong hearts and lungs, healthy bones, and a healthy body. ***Latest research indicates it even correlates with a healthy brain, leading to better ability to focus, improved memory, and enhanced cognitive development. Scientists even report that physically fit children show overall better school performance.*** A person's ability to control their large body parts that enable walking, running, kicking, sitting upright, lifting, and throwing depends on both muscle tone and strength, which gets stronger and more flexible with exercise and an active life style. On the other hand, lack of exercise and an immobile lifestyle will cause a person's body to be weak and underdeveloped, resulting in poor brain function as well.

Fine Motor Coordination

Eye-hand coordination, also called fine motor coordination, relates to the ability of the eyes to control the fine muscle movement of the hands and fingers and enables small, precise movements of the fingers, hands, toes, and tongues. Control of these body parts helps fingers manipulate crayons, pencils, scissors, and blocks, as well as fastening, tying shoes, or picking up small objects. ***Early development of fine motor skills has been connected with high achievement in math, science and reading, and is correlated with children's readiness for school. Scientists even report that advanced fine motor skills are an early prediction of school success.***

There is excellent supporting information on the Internet that parents should read so they can understand how vitally important playing is to the development of their child's brain. Below are statements you can enter in the search bar that will bring you to several websites. Hopefully they will convince you of the importance of getting rid of the television and computer games that are keeping your child's brain from developing to its fullest potential.

The importance of child's play to brain development.
Brain development and physical movement.
The connection between motor skills and cognition.

The Importance of Play!

Adults who care about keeping their bodies and brains healthy concentrate on eating nutritious food and exercise. They have active lifestyles and may participate in sports, jogging, or work out in gyms regularly. Children cannot do these things on their own, so how do they develop healthy minds and bodies? ***By playing! They were meant to play! The way children play and with whom are precursors to all subsequent development. The mental and physical skills children develop during early play experiences are essential to their social, emotional, cognitive, and physical well-being. Child development experts recommend children have no less than 60 minutes and up to several hours of physical activity each day.***

Once children pass the play age, they won't learn these skills anywhere else; they're not taught from books, nor are they taught in school. Such skills must be learned through experience gained from play. In later years, adults may develop some of these skills, but it must be through interacting with others. and the quality of these skills will never be what could have been acquired through playing.

There are two types of play: structured and unstructured. Each group helps children develop specialized skills which need to be developed while they are maturing, from preschool through adolescence. ***Child development experts say that specific play in children's formative years is the most beneficial and important stage of their lives.***

Unstructured Play

This type of play is unplanned. It's called free play, because the kids instigate the play which can be anything they want, both physical and mental. Creative play activities are indispensable for development of both gross and fine coordination. There are no rules, no set ways to play, and no one to tell children what to do or how to do it. Parents may provide playthings or they'll fashion their own.

During free play children develop creativity, imagination, and independence; they build self-confidence and self-esteem, learn self-regulation, and problem solving skills; they begin to make their own decisions and learn about consequences. Numerous studies equate play with logic, higher IQ scores, problem solving, and language skills. By having friends during play, children also develop social skills: how to make friends, cooperate, share, take turns, play fair, and they learn to resolve conflicts. Whether they're playing dress up, playing doctor and nurse, or making up their own games, kids are learning leadership qualities and valuable ways to interact with each other.

Children need friendships so they can learn about feelings, how to communicate, and solve problems. If there are no siblings or children living close by, parents could establish friendships with other mothers and invite their children over to play. They could also make arrangements with other parents to take turns babysitting the kids on *Park Day* when they take their school-age kids to the park to play while the others have free time. *A major setback for children who enter kindergarten is having reached that age without enough interaction with other children.*

Structured Play

This play is the opposite of free play and can be either physical or mental. *It involves children having fun by learning how to do things. It includes organized sports, physical education programs, and supervised play led by adults such as a parent, coach or scout leader, even an older sibling.* This can involve learning to swim or play baseball, Simon Says, spelling games, assembling model airplanes, or coloring by number…anything that has rules or directions to follow and results in learning of some kind. When children enter school they begin to get more involved in structured activities and will be involved in both types of play until they're too old for free play.

Becoming accomplished at learning to do something like playing tennis or swimming builds children's confidence and self-esteem. Team activities teach sportsmanship, cooperation and communication. Children learn how to abide by the rules, how to be fair and to behave when they win or lose a game. Very importantly, structured activities that involve moving muscles and large parts of the body increase coordination and sets the stage for active adult lifestyles.

Younger children generally like the unstructured play because they have more fun, but they also enjoy getting the attention of adults who teach them fun things to do. Make certain the time and place are consistently available and supply the items the children can use during their play. It shouldn't be too difficult to find a balance between the two types. One can differentiate between them by remembering that unstructured means *free play* while structured means *how to play*. Toddlers and preschoolers are too little for organized sports or advanced teaching activities, so you can concentrate on encouraging them to just play. Most structured play activities that require use of major muscles are played outside, unless they're doing somersaults, playing Leapfrog on the front room carpet, or jumping on an old mattress inside, while unstructured activities that support the fine motor skills are usually played inside.

Although wonderful parent/child contact time can be through playing with your children, it's not your responsibility to always play with them, tell them what games to play, or teach them how to play. Kids were born to play! **If you keep them away from**

television, they'll have nothing else to do except what comes natural to them. Just provide them with the materials and play things when necessary. Usually, if you leave the kids alone they will find ways to play and things to play with. They're so fascinating and creative! I remember my kids' creative play: grocery shopping with doll buggies as a grocery cart, a toy cash register, and my canned and packaged goods to purchase; a veterinarian treating their dog, a priest in church giving blessings, and distributing communion. They made trains with my kitchen chairs, and tents with blankets draped over the sofa or clothes lines. They always found something to do with whatever objects were available to use.

Other than home chores, schoolwork, or important places to go and be, children's free time should be spent playing in some form, whether it's with art, crafts, or quiet games while inside, or strenuous physical activity outdoors. After school and on weekends they should play outside during the day; even when it's cold, bundle them up and send them out for a reasonable length of time. There should always be a place to play indoors, even if it's in the front room.

It's very likely that many of today's parents are the products of too much screen time and not enough play when they were growing up, so they may not be familiar with many beneficial play activities in which their children can be involved. In the remainder of this chapter, I have listed numerous play things and activities that will give you ideas as to what you can provide for your child that will satisfy both types of play and for both indoor and outdoor activities. Kids usually learn from other kids, but when they don't have companions they may not know how to play many of the games. If you don't know either, google *Games for different ages on the Internet.* You can also find many other activities such as, games for preschoolers to play indoors, games to build coordination in six-to ten-year-olds, or card games for older children.

Keep Your Kids Busy and Healthy

Kids don't need expensive, commercial toys that will break, or they'll soon become bored with. If left alone, they'll find ways to be active and create their own fun activities. Don't ever throw anything out that could be turned into creative play things for toddlers-to twelve-year-olds.

Here are some items you can provide that children will use to get healthy exercise while they create their own play:

- blankets

- old sheets
- pillows
- mats
- old clothes, including hats, shoes, jewelry
- old mattresses (ideal if you have a place to store it such as basement or garage)
- large exercise ball they can roll on
- balls of different sizes
- bean bags
- boxes of all kinds: shipping, toothpaste, vitamin, food, oatmeal, cereal
- appliance boxes for building tunnels, making cabins, forts, etc. (with parents help)
- paper towel/bathroom tissue rolls
- feed or grain sacks they can put their feet in and hop around
- thick tape to put on the floor in designs they can balance on while walking
- plastic buckets
- plastic containers: vitamin bottles, milk and juice bottles, coffee containers
- wood scraps (make certain the edges are sanded so child can't get slivers)
- water and paint brushes when warm outside
- sand, dirt (for mud)
- sidewalk chalk
- sponges
- measuring cups

Babies and Toddlers – Unstructured Stage

Since babies aren't old enough to be taught ways to play or follow directions, the motions they are able to perform would be classified as *unstructured* which promote their gross motor coordination. Until babies and toddlers are old enough to function on their own, parents can help their development in the following ways:

- Place colorful scarves and mobiles over their beds which they can hit and kick.
- Help them to sit up by grasping their hands and gently pulling them into a sitting position.
- Help them roll over.
- Exercise them by gently bending their knees and touching their elbows. They love this!
- Play Patty Cake and Peek-a-Boo.
- Entice them to crawl to toys placed around the room.

- Help them to stand up next to furniture such as a sofa, foot rest, or end tables.
- Place large and small pillows around the room for them to crawl round and over.
- Place them in a high chair and give them objects to manipulate.

Here are some toys babies and toddlers can grasp and play with:

- rattles
- colored scarves
- shakers
- rubber blocks
- smooth balls
- squeeze toys
- noise makers
- riding toys
- empty plastic bottles
- stacking cups and rings

Preschool Children – Unstructured Play

Here are some of the most common toys and activities that may be used in children's free play. Be sure to have an abundant supply of items from which the child can select. Most of these may be purchased reasonably from Walmart. Be selective when looking for birthday and holiday gifts that will contribute to the child's body or eye-hand coordination. Remember, *free play* means the child is left alone to play creatively, without any rules or directions.

drawing	tricycles
popsicle sticks	wagons
balloons	push/pull toys
scribbling	toy brooms
using scissors	chalk and chalk boards
coloring their own drawings	toy dishes
brush painting	shovels and buckets
finger painting	dolls and buggies
play dough	play kitchenettes
modeling clay	flannel boards
finger puppets	peg boards

building blocks	toy trains and cars
balls of all sizes	rocks and sticks
boxes of all sizes	sand and mud
water and sponges	adult paint brushes
lacing cards	plastic figures
stringing beads	building blocks

Following are unstructured activities that are strongly related to the gross motor coordination of children. See to it that they play outside for at least an hour or more every day. If you provide the time, place, and materials, they will play naturally and get the exercise their bodies need. Children are so interesting! If you observe them you'll find that they will spend most of their time running and chasing, which is the best exercise they can get. Try your best to find playmates for them. They get the best exercise when they have someone to romp with.

grass rolling	throwing
summersaults	running
chasing	marching
climbing	dancing
walking	tumbling
kicking	clapping
hopping	jumping
catching	bouncing

School-Age children – Unstructured

When children begin school, they continue to be involved with the same preschool unstructured activities as listed above, and will move on to those more advanced, such as:

monkey bars
hop scotch
jump rope
sliding
swinging
bicycling
scooters
skate boards
roller skating

leap frog
paddle ball

Preschool Through School-Age Children – Structured Activities

As children grow older many will continue to be creative in unstructured activities, such as art, language and science. They also become capable of learning to follow directions and follow rules, which leads to interesting hobbies and healthy adult life styles. Following are a number of games and sporting activities which children are taught, or that have directions to follow that are created, designed, or supervised by adults that your older children will enjoy:

color by number books	Red Light, Green Light
work books	Mother May I
puzzles	Kick the Can
knitting	Hide and Go Seek
beading	Blind Man's Bluff
Dominos	Simon Says
Tinker Toys	Red Rover
Checkers	Pool
Monopoly	Internet action games
Pick-Up-sticks	relay races
Log Cabin	hand clap games
card games	kick ball
board games	volley ball
spelling games	gymnastics
math games	tumbling
vocabulary games	softball
model airplanes	swimming
ceramics	basketball
jacks	leap frog

Hobbies and Extracurricular Activities for Older Children

How do today's older children pass their time if they're not interested in sports and they're too old to play? Usually they watch television, or they become addicted to their smartphones. What a shame! There are so many hobbies and healthy activities that will continue the development of the skills they learned during their earlier years. Many childhood skills will also carry over into advanced enjoyment during the adult years. ***Participation in any of these activities will greatly enhance mental development as well as vocabulary, confidence, and self-esteem.*** It is not necessary for parents to be involved in any of these activities other than support in the form of encouragement and cooperation in supplying the child with materials, finances, transportation, and attendance at related events.

Many of the following activities are taught through high schools as well as churches, 4H, the YMCA and YWCA. Some cities have education or art centers which teach multiple classes of various interests. Your city's Chamber of Commerce may be aware of places offering classes which you may pursue for your older children. If you don't keep your children busy they'll waste their precious child-development years.

dance	photography
music	stamp collecting
voice	ceramics
drama	woodworking
sewing	dog training
cooking	gardening/house plants
choir	Boy/Girl Scouts

Remember, when you allow your children to spend hours idly watching television or other mindless activities, important parts of their brains go undeveloped, which will affect their entire adult lives.

Just turn off the television and take away the cell phones and computers and let your children's brains and bodies develop. Play and exercise will bring them cognitive, social, emotional, and physical benefit.

Chapter 5

THE HOME ENVIRONMENT CONDUCIVE TO LEARNING

"Parents are prone to give their children everything except the one thing they need most, and that is time; time for listening, time for understanding, time for helping and time for guiding. It sounds simple, but in reality it is the most difficult and most sacrificial task of parenthood."

Emma K. Hulbert

If I were to prioritize the area of most importance to children's development, I would select the family environment as one of the highest. ***What children experience in their home while growing up will determine their future success or failure, and will be a part of them for the rest of their lives.*** We are all products of our home environment, and what we learn from our homes, good or bad, we carry over to the homes we establish for our own children. Providing your children with a home where the family spends time loving, sharing, contributing, and learning together will produce children who feel secure and have a strong sense of belonging, prerequisites to developing good self-esteem. Their brains will grow to potential, and they will become fully capable of achieving success in their lives.

There are many ways to create homes with enriched learning environments. They don't have to be in upper class neighborhoods filled with elaborate furniture and all the newest toys and fashions, nor must the parents have college degrees. Parents of various backgrounds and financial status are all capable of creating home environments that are equipped with the provisions that are conducive to their children's learning. With a little bit of planning and learning on the parents' part, they can create a family atmosphere that will lay the groundwork for the development of their children's confidence and self-esteem. This can easily be done and it doesn't have to be all at once...just in the course of daily living.

As with most other suggestions in this book, ***the recommendations in this chapter are achieved simply through daily contact parents have with their children, rules they establish, and the quality of the home environment.***

Television – The Downfall of Education and Family Life

Homes with children cannot be learning friendly when the television is on all hours of the day and night. Child development specialists recommend there be no television before the age of two, and one hour a day for those from two to school-age, provided the programs are of high-quality content, and that parents watch them with the child. This is very reasonable, especially during the day when preschool children have a lot of time at home. Be sure to check the Internet for beneficial programs for them to watch, such as with numbers, the alphabet, social interacting, dancing, and singing, but it's an absolute must that you watch with the young child. It's very tempting to let him watch himself while you get some work done; however, keep in mind, you are the link between your child's learning and just sitting idly and watching the screen. You must be the teacher.

For the school-age children, specialists recommend *no more than two hours of viewing per day.* My question to them is, when? This may be all right for summer months and weekends, when the children have a lot of time on their hands. *Viewing worthwhile programs, no more than two hours per day, may provide a healthy balance between chores, outside play, and some educational activities; however, they should not be allowed to watch television on school nights, which should be devoted to homework, bathing, and getting clothes and things ready for school the next day.*

Following are several problems television creates for parents which they have difficulty overcoming:

- Finding worthwhile programs for the kids to watch.
- Finding time to watch programs with the kids.
- Kids changing the channel to other programs without the parents' knowledge.
- The strong temptation to let the kids watch television so they can have peace and quiet.

For these reasons, I recommend that there be a no television policy in homes on school nights, and then just two hours of strictly monitored television on weekends. There are numerous other activities described in this book that are fun and conducive to learning, instead of letting the children sit idly watching screens that have no beneficial value.

Unrestricted Smartphones

Smartphones are the primary mode of socializing among school kids today. I don't have anything nice to say about them except that they're great for the convenience of parents and children calling each other, when needed. My major complaint is that some children are using them to bully vulnerable students in such cruel ways that are causing them extreme anxiety, even to the point of committing suicide.

Parents should know their children's phone passwords and make themselves aware, daily, of the messages and pictures their children are sending and receiving. Children should not be given phone privacy until they are out of high school. Here is when good character training is mandatory. Parents should be aware that kindness is not a trait that children are born with… that if they don't teach their children to be kind and compassionate, how to empathize with those who are being bullied, and how wrong it is, they will very likely follow their peers and take part in bullying other students.

Unlimited use of cell phones is also severely damaging to family life and parent/child relationships. Parents should have strict rules about when and where their kids may use their cell phones. If allowed, they will continuously text from morning to night, during meals and homework, while at church and even in bed, until well after midnight, when they finally fall asleep.

I suggest the following restrictions, as well as a lock box in which to put the phones when their use is forbidden. You should not hesitate to forbid their use altogether for days or weeks, as consequences for breaking the rules or not fulfilling their responsibilities.

- before breakfast
- during meals
- when in the company of adults
- while in church or shopping
- after dinner, unless all chores, homework and school prep are done
- after lights out
- limit to two hours a day usage
- no cell phones for children below sixth grade

Organization

Organization is a skill that is mandatory for children to learn at home. The disorganized child is a poor student: he can't find his homework, forgets his books, and never has pencils. He doesn't know where his lunch money is and doesn't know where he put his take-home notes. I spent hours with these students, showing them how to organize their desks and book bags, where to put pencils and books, and how to use bookmarks. I would give them folders in which to place take-home notes and corrected assignments, and together we discarded papers and things that should have been thrown out weeks earlier; however, in a few days the child would regress to his own messy, disorganized self again. The time I gave him could not help him overcome the disorganized habits that he formed at home. *Children must be raised in an organized environment, otherwise they'll be disorganized for life.* Here's how to give them a start in the right direction:

- Almost every home with children has a toy box where all toys are kept, mixed up. The children will pull the box out and dump it, play for a while, then throw everything back in until the next time. The toys in this box are the first things to organize.

- Each child's bedroom should have shelves. Everything in the toy box needs to be categorized and have its place. Books, games, stuffed animals, and toys should be on the shelves; smaller items such as blocks, Dominos, Lego, doll clothes and accessories, and small, plastic figures should be stored in smaller boxes or even zip lock bags and placed on the shelves.

- Each child's bedroom should have a closet with a clothes rack within reach on which to hang up her clothes and a small set of shelves on which to place her shoes.

- Each child should have her own dresser in which to keep underclothes, socks, and whatever else that needs a place. Everything should be folded and in its proper place, and there should be a hamper in which to place dirty clothes.

- There should also be shelves close to where the child leaves for school. School things should be placed on these shelves before the child goes to bed, ready to grab in the morning when she leaves for school. Organized book bags should be complete with books, pencils, homework, lunch money, and notes.

- Besides the kitchen table, there should be another all-purpose table somewhere in the home, preferably in the family room, that would be used for homework and art. I used a door slab propped up on each end by metal file cabinets. The table is perfect for art projects, and supplies can be stored in the file cabinets.

- There should be a sturdy pencil sharpener in a permanent location and a pencil box or jar for sharpened pencils, easily available for the child to put in her book bag in preparation for school.

- A wastebasket should be next to the table.

- A note basket should be placed on or near the homework table in which the child is to place all notes and corrected take-home papers as soon as he comes home. Parents should check this box each evening for important notes or corrected papers they are supposed to see. Those they must sign and send back should be given directly to the child to put in his school bag so they won't be forgotten.

- A large desk calendar pinned to the kitchen wall on which to keep track of each family member's appointments and activities, such as doctor, dentist, lunches, meetings, teacher's conferences, after school activities, car repair, library book

- due dates, etc. Color-coding each child's activities makes it easier for Mom to keep everything separate. Children should have their own supplemental calendar and the responsibility of keeping track of their personal activities.

- Every family with young children should have a wall where they may display their art work and school papers that deserve special mention. The wall in my home was in our kitchen so we could comment on the papers during dinner. It's great to have another wall on which they may pin large art projects, such as landscapes, forests, mountains, animals, Indian villages, etc. They should also be allowed to draw on it with colored chalk and paint with water colors. Cleaning the wall should be the child's responsibility. Art walls are worth the pleasure they provide.

Educational Materials

- A large U.S. map – See if your local Chamber of Commerce has one, or perhaps you can get one free on the Internet. Pin the map on the wall in an appropriate place where it can be referred to often. The kitchen or family room wall is great. You may want to laminate the map so you can wipe fingerprints, and it will not wear out. It's easy to laminate with clear contact paper you can get at Walmart. Use the map when you read or hear of something of interest in another city or state.

- City, state and county maps – These maps would be used to pinpoint various places of interest, such as city hall, courthouses, shopping centers, parks, and streets.

- A large world globe – This should be situated somewhere close to the television set. Children could learn more Geography at home than they do at school just by tracking interesting events the family hears about on television, or reads about in the newspapers.

- Dictionaries – Both adult and children's in hardback form should be available for the parents and young child to use together.

- A child's picture dictionary – This is by far the easiest way to teach your preschooler and early grade child vocabulary words that are far too difficult to explain without pictures.

- Adult and child Thesauri – These books contain a treasury of synonyms which

- are excellent for teaching school-age children more sophisticated vocabulary words when writing. Small paperbacks are very affordable.

- Encyclopedias – These are expensive books, but so valuable to have. They're filled with wonderful colored pictures, diagrams, illustrations and explanations that will turn children on to investigative reading to satisfy their curiosity. I recommend World Book for elementary children. Make certain the set you purchase is at the child's level, yet may still be used as the child ages. See what is available on the Internet. You can put them on your wish list and save up for them. Try an ad in your Penny Saver. It would be worth driving a few hundred miles to a surrounding city to get a good buy on a used set.

- A family computer on which to look up information, dictionary words, or synonyms instead of using books.

Positive Role Models

Children will imitate everything they see you do. Make certain they see examples of behavior that you want them to imitate such as:

- use of the dictionary
- use of the Thesaurus
- looking for information on the Internet
- involvement in self-improvement projects
- reading for enjoyment
- reading the daily newspapers
- taking a college class
- reading directions

Books in the Home

If you don't remember the "*500 Book*" study conducted by Mariah Evans referenced in Chapter One, "Listen to the Experts," be sure to go back and read it again. ***Based on data she and her assistants collected from 73,249 families, most children raised in homes that had 500 books graduated from college with a Bachelors' Degree and earned $21,185 a year more than those who didn't go to college.***

Upon first hearing this, a parent might be overwhelmed, visualizing walls of books throughout their home, and wonder how they could possibly model this study. In reality, if parents habitually read to their children as recommended and are readers themselves, it would be quite simple. Beginning when the child is one year old, suppose you purchase just one new book a month. That would add up to 120 books in 10 years. How many more would you purchase if you had two or three children? But you could accumulate many more books from thrift stores and garage sales, as well as gifts for holidays and birthdays. Now 500 books sounds more realistic.

Children are delighted to receive books as gifts, especially when they know you will be reading to them. Each time an occasion arises to buy gifts such as birthdays, Christmas, Easter, or Valentine's Day, make certain one or two of the gifts is a book. If your children have grandparents, aunts or uncles that buy for them, it isn't too forward to ask them to purchase books instead of other expensive gifts. Below is an assortment of highly enjoyable books that your children would be delighted to have, especially if parents read to them:

- Colorful picture books for the early toddler to teach names of animals and objects
- The *Joy Witt Berry* books teach preschool children about difficult behaviors such as being greedy, messy, rude, lazy, wasteful, throwing tantrums, crying, and bedtime.
- *Mother Goose Rhymes* and tongue-twisters
- *Dr. Seuss* stories are some of the most delightful books available for preschool to grade three children who will want you to read these over and over to them.
- "Read-a-Long" stories with tapes are great for early grade independent reading and listening.
- I *Can Read* books for preschoolers are great for learning sight words.
- Books about science of any kind: animals, insects, snakes, ocean life, volcanoes, earthquakes, the human body, amphibians, and spiders
- Books about prehistoric animals, green things, ocean life, insects, and world places
- High interest, low vocabulary books come in a series, such as western, mysteries, and animals. These are great for older children who are having difficulty reading, for example books with stories that would interest an older fifth grade child who may be reading at a third grade level.
- National Geographic magazines for children from third through middle grades
- Classics for the middle grade child such as, *Lassie, Call of the Wild, Red Badge of Courage* and *Old Yeller.*
- Children's magazines you can subscribe to that would be delivered monthly.

- Readers Digest has neat true-to-life stories parents can read to middle grade children.
- Subscriptions to children's magazines such as Ranger Rick, Lady Bug, or Boys' and Girls' Life.

Money Making Projects

Don't feel bad if you have to pinch pennies just to make ends meet, and never have enough left to buy educational materials. I can remember starting in May to save a little bit of money out of each paycheck to buy my children's back-to-school clothes in September. And our children had to take sack lunches, because we couldn't afford to buy school lunches for three kids every day. We didn't have much money for buying books, but we spent a lot of time at the library. *Besides borrowing from the library, there are ways the education-minded family can find used books they can afford to purchase, as well as earn the money to purchase new ones. All you need is the desire and willingness to put yourselves out a little bit. Here are numerous ways…take your pick:*

- Open a special account at the bank for book money only and deposit extra money in it whenever you can. Even if it's only $5.00 a month, it's a great way to save for the valued encyclopedias.

- Most cities have consignment shops where you may take your good used clothing you can't wear anymore. They'll sell them for you, keep a percentage and give you the rest. You may make as much as $5.00 for an outgrown child's jacket. Even $.50 for a pair of trousers, added to .50 cents each for shirts, blouses, shoes, etc. will build up your book fund.

- Advertising in your city's Penny Saver or free online advertising are the best ways I know of to find real bargains for good, used books, magazines, the world globe, and other educational items. A simple ad such as, "I want to buy good, used children's books," may bring you dozens.

- Garage sales are always great moneymakers. Some people have a garage sale every six months to a year. A good way to get items really cheap is to shop other people's sales just before closing. Most people contribute everything they have left at the end of their sale to charity, and would gladly sell you anything for a fraction of what they were asking. Then you can sell them for fractions more, plus sell your own outgrown or unwanted things. It will all add up.

- There's good money in selling used baby clothes and furniture. Some people never buy any new items for their babies, because they can buy second hand items that are practically new. Be an early bird at garage sales, and buy any baby toys, books, or furniture that are in good condition. Have a continuous want ad running in the Thrifty Nickel for toys, books and baby items. Accumulate them until you have enough for a giant baby item sale right before Christmas, or sell them in bundles on eBay.

- Shop the Goodwill or thrift stores for good, used children's books.

- Ask your children's school principal if the school would sponsor a used book sale.

Family Discussions

Family meal time can be a nightmare, as I remember so well: children arguing and complaining, parents shouting, threatening, and sending obnoxious kids away from the table. I don't think any family with children can escape dinner-time turmoil, but it doesn't have to be that way. ***Time spent eating meals together can be of the highest quality. It can be the only time when everyone is together to really communicate. Parents and children can share things of interest that happened in school or throughout their day, but you must set down rules and strictly abide by them, and if the children disobey, they should be sent to their room without finishing their meal.***

Begin by teaching the rules for conversation, such as don't interrupt, don't speak with your mouth full, take turns, and listen politely to others. Before long, you will progress to a somewhat happy and semi-relaxed family social hour, mostly free of scolding and reprimands. Here are some possible table topics:

- hearing the little ones relate something about a game they played, with whom they played, or a story that was read to them at preschool or kindergarten
- hearing the school children share something that happened in school, something they learned, did during recess, or the highlight of their day
- complimenting the children for doing particularly well at something, such as good grades, keeping their bedroom clean, or being more polite than usual
- parents relating events in their day that may be interesting or relevant to the child
- discussions of current events that would interest the children
- highlighting each member of the family, so other members may say something

- nice about that person, such as her manners, how she showed kindness to someone, or was helpful in some way
- taking turns sharing something nice they did that day for someone else

Vocabulary Enrichment

This activity is so simple that all a family needs to do is become aware of interesting words they can post on the wall and encourage the family to use when they're together. Children and adults can learn hundreds of words from early grades to high school.

Begin when the child is school-age, and continue for as long as you can keep everyone motivated. Just two words a month will add up to 24 in a year. *Just one a month would be great! Don't worry if you can't be consistent. Even every now and then would work.*

Select a word that would appeal to the child, depending on age, or help her select one. Print it on a 2" x 8" strip of tagboard and tape it to the kitchen wall where the family will see it often. Challenge the entire family to use the word as often as possible, for a week. Find ways to relate it to present situations. For example, if the word is *murmur*, you might playfully chastise the child for not speaking loudly enough by saying, "Speak up, Stephie! When you murmur we can't hear you!" Then mumble something to her so she can't understand you and say, "This is how you sound when you *murmur*." Other words might be *ravenous* and *appetite*. When you sit down to eat dinner you might comment that you have a *ravenous appetite.*

Look for words that are fun and interesting! Good sources for new vocabulary words are the Reader's Digest, the newspaper or other magazines. For example, in one Reader's Digest there was a story about "Luke, the Lackadaisical Labrador," which is about a dog that became listless when the children went to school. Another appealing story was "Midnight, the Protective Feline," about a cat who saved the life of a baby choking in bed by meowing into the baby's monitor. The vocabulary words could be *feline, monitor, protective,* and *lackadaisical.* Offer to put a nickel or dime in the family bank designated for family pizza each time the word is used.

Right to Read

Have a weekly (or more often) period when everyone in the family spends time reading something of interest such as newspaper, magazines, the Bible, comic books, library book, or directions for assembling something. The gist of the period is that every one has the right to enjoy reading during the designated time, without interruption. This should be serious reading for 30 minutes, in complete silence. Everyone use the restroom first, then no moving around, no phones, or talking.

My students loved this period in the classroom, and begged me to extend it. Their favorite places to read were under their desks, or sprawled out on the floor, and in corners. If you can't get them to settle down quickly, count to twenty, by which time everyone must be reading or send those not ready to their room.

This would be a great diversion when the kids are arguing or bored and looking for something to do. Just declare it "Right to Read" time and you will have peace and quiet for a while. You can even beg out from participating if you have something important to do while the kids are quiet.

Newspaper (good for summer vacation)

Newspapers are one of the most versatile and inexpensive reading tools available to the family. Some even have a syndicated children's supplement that features articles, puzzles, and stories especially for young readers. If parents have no other reading materials available, they will do very well just by using the daily newspaper for their family's reading activities. Never throw a newspaper out until it's in shreds. Beginning with the early school child:

- Look for large headlines to make it easier for her to see individual letters. Circle or highlight with marking pen, letters of the alphabet she knows. Cut them out to paste in her alphabet scrapbook. Look for large letters with which to spell her name and other relevant words, such as ball, mommy or baby.
- Let her circle or highlight the easy sight words she needs to learn for reading, such as the, and, this, said, that.
- Cut out entire words to be put together to form sentences in her scrapbook.
- School children can look for sentences that contain punctuation marks and highlight them, which will reinforce language skills they are being taught in school such as exclamation points, question marks, and quotation marks.
- Have her make a list of contractions she sees, and write the two words the contraction represents.
- A scavenger hunt is a fun way of teaching the older child about the newspaper. Preview the newspaper and give her a list of items for her search. Help her with ones she can't find.

- As an incentive, offer the child a nickel for each item she finds.

Some ideas for things to find:

- a photograph of a child and the caption
- a sports statistic about a high school team in your city
- the prediction of your city's temperature
- a picture of a dog
- a bed or dresser advertised in the miscellaneous for sale column
- picture of a new truck or car
- an article about the president
- a recipe
- the name of a plumber for hire

Library

Libraries are a one-stop resource for awesome fun and entertainment for entire families. You'll find a variety of materials and programs, puzzles, videos, music, and books to check out, as well as exciting learning centers equipped with puppets, blocks, Legos, and computers. Some branches even have plays, story times, and book clubs. Make certain you get a calendar of activities which usually change every month.

It may be difficult for families to frequent libraries during school months, but be sure to take advantage of what they have to offer during the summer when children are bored and have too much time on their hands. ***The library could be their major source of summer time pleasure.***

- Start taking your children to the library when they're toddlers. Get them their own library card when old enough. Celebrate with a cake and special family time. Make certain they accept the responsibilities that go with borrowing books: keep them in their proper place, don't bend or tear pages, and don't read them while eating or drinking. Give them a calendar on which to keep a record of return dates, and teach them to remind you when they're due.

- At first, all young children will like books like *Dr. Seuss, Nursery Rhymes, Barney,* and other animated stories which are on display to browse through and select. But as they get older they will develop interests in favorites, such as detective, mysteries, sports, animals, and so on. Help your children develop their own interests; show them how to use the library computer to find books, and

- encourage them to ask the librarian for assistance.

- When your child selects books that interest her, if she is not an accomplished reader she may select books that are too difficult. Before letting her check out books, you should do a quick test by having her read a paragraph from the book. If she comes upon three or more words she doesn't know, then it's too difficult for her to read independently, which may cause her to lose interest. Help her find books at her level, but still check out the ones she wants that are a bit too difficult so you can read them together.

- Don't assume that your child will take time from her play to read. You will need to provide the time such as after lunch, rest time or a consistent "Right to Read" time. When she becomes an accomplished reader this won't be necessary, because she'll probably get hooked on an interesting book and read on her own.

- Finally, be certain to check books out yourselves, even if it's just one. Remember, your children copy what they observe you doing. If you don't read and show an interest in the library for your own pleasure, your attempts at helping them develop an interest may go by the wayside in their future.

Family Garden.

After just a few weeks of summer freedom, the kids get bored and start nagging you for something to do. You can't make them read and do chores all day, so you're tempted to give in, and let them watch too much television. What else can you do with them? Consider a family garden. There's no project more enjoyable, educational, and rewarding, which will carry over into their adult lives. It wouldn't take all of their time, but at least it would be part of a variety of healthy activities to keep them busy, such as reading, arts and crafts, a few hours of television, playing outside, chores, and a garden.

I suggest you begin on a very small scale, when the kids are in preschool or in early grades. Just use large planters for lettuce, spinach, and perhaps tomato and cucumber plants in separate containers. This way you can get them accustomed to watering, a bit of weeding, and the excitement of harvesting. These will be enough to motivate them to wanting a larger garden.

When they're a few years older, graduate to a small patch in the ground, perhaps ten feet square. Let this be their garden, with as little help from you as possible. Be sure to help them search the library and Internet for information about how to plant a gar den that will help explain the different vocabulary and skills. After all is finished, it shouldn't take more than thirty minutes a day to maintain, which will increase to perhaps a half hour in the mornings and evenings. There is so much to learn: new skills and vocabulary, as well as self-discipline, responsibility, feelings of satisfaction, pride, and truly a sense of belonging to the family. The "garden bug" will follow them well into adulthood.

Following are numerous garden related skills and vocabulary words that may be found in library books, or on the Internet:

- starting your own seed
- cultivating
- the importance of sunlight
- composting
- early vegetables and fruits
- fertilizing
- thinning
- weeding
- herbicide
- natural insect control
- insecticides
- flowers that attract butterflies
- lady bugs
- pollination
- harvesting
- reading recipes
- preparing food
- food value

Dancing

Don't let yourself be so busy that you never have time to just plain have fun with your children.

Family members who work hard day after day with no recreation become stressed and tend to not get along. Children argue and fight, resist obeying rules, and doing their responsibilities. Parents lose patience and shout and punish. You all need a diversion from working, chores, studying, and obeying rules. There should be a healthy bal ance between work and play, but sometimes it's difficult to find activities that give the needed recreation often enough. Why not consider dancing? I mean everybody, not just the kids. Family dancing in the recreation room, front room, basement, even the kitchen or outside. Wherever and whenever its practical and possible. Even consider playing music on the patio in summer and inviting friends to join.

You'll be surprised at what you find if you research the *value of dancing* on the Internet. I found too many benefits to repeat in this chapter. **Some are coordination, balance, flexibility, mobility, enjoyment, self-confidence, and self-esteem. There are even a number of brain skills that would be extremely conducive to your children's learning. Some of them are observation, repetition, modeling, and brain memory. If you need convincing about how dancing and learning go together, research "The educational benefits of dancing," on the Internet.**

Don't wait until your children are older; begin when they're babies. They love it when parents cuddle them and gently sway back and forth and dance slowly to soft music. When my kids were old enough to hold like a dance partner, they'd scream with delight when we bounced and swirled to lively music, then we'd put our faces together and dance slowly. They'd cry for more.

When they're old enough to walk, begin teaching them to move and sway creatively to the music. There should be no special way to move. What's wonderful about pre-schoolers is they are completely uninhibited. They'll move to their heart's content, not caring who is watching or how they look. Children love to march and clap their hands to music. Clapping and marching can be a prelude to feeling the rhythm of dance music. Help your child feel the rhythm of the music with a toy drum, or by clapping your hands and stomping your feet. Let your hair down and start getting into the hand clapping, hip shaking, wiggling and bouncing kind of dancing. Learn to dance the Macarena, do the Hokey Pokey, learn Hip Hop and Line Dancing.

Again, check the Internet for videos of kids dancing and having a good time. Play the videos when you're together, for the kids when you're busy, or when the kids are bored and need something to do. Many Adults are inhibited and shy because they missed out on fun like this when they were children. Besides dancing with your family at home, you may prevent this from happening to your children by enrolling them in dance lessons, such as Tap, Swing, Modern, Western and Line. How sad that most parents think dance lessons are just for girls. Nothing will build confidence more or discourage shyness and inhibitions as much as dancing and performing in front of an audience.

While reviewing this chapter, you will see that all of the suggestions can be implemented through daily contact with your children. You just need to create your family living style based on intermingling with each other, setting up rules, and providing good role models for them to imitate.

Chapter 6

....

RESPONSIBILITY:
THE KEY INGREDIENT OF SUCCESS

"In the final analysis, the one quality that all successful people have is the ability to take on responsibility."

Michael Korda

Learning to be responsible for one's home and personal needs is the first step up the ladder of success. Mother should be free to perform her important personal and family chores while the kids learn responsibility for themselves and contribute to a stable home environment. However, ***children aren't born with these skills...they must be taught how to do their share and fend for themselves. It won't be easy or happen overnight, and it will take years of time and patience, but in the long run you will have a happy, organized home life with everyone doing their share while contributing toward their future independence.*** You need to formulate a workable plan to follow at which you can be consistent and well-organized. Following are my suggestions to use as a guide. You will most likely want to change, delete and add skills suitable to your own family.

Personal Responsibilities for Preschool to K

You should give your children responsibility according to their ability. A child who can walk should be taught to pick up his dirty clothes and put them in the laundry basket, clean up spills, and place his toys and books back where they belong. This is the foundation for all future responsible actions. As children get older, their personal responsibilities should increase. ***Two to three years is a good time to start. Children this young will need help with most of the listed skills, but they should all be mastered by Kindergarten age. One of the frustrations of teachers is that they must help their students do things they should have learned at home.***

A.M.

- Get out of bed when called.
- Use the bathroom and come to breakfast.
- Help set the table.
- Put dirty dishes in the dishwasher.
- Get dressed, make the bed.
- Brush teeth.
- Put shoes on and tie them.
- Zip jacket zippers.
- Button shirt and jacket buttons.
- Put on jackets, caps, and mittens.
- Put boots on and take off.
- Remove jacket and store mittens in sleeves or pockets.
- Hang up jacket.

P.M.

- Put toys and other belongings away.
- Undress and turn socks, panties, or shorts right side out.
- Turn sleeves and pant legs right side out.
- Empty pockets and put all dirty clothes in hamper.
- Put shoes and clean socks by the bed for next day.
- Set out clothes to wear the next day.
- Bathe, with help, then rinse sink or tub.
- Hang towel and washcloth, and put on pajamas.
- Brush teeth, rinse sink, put brush in holder.
- Be ready on time for bedtime story.

Personal Responsibilities from Kindergarten on Up

Following are personal responsibilities that everyone should have. ***By the time children are in sixth grade they should own most of these.*** They're listed from easy, for preschoolers, to more difficult, for upper grades.

- Clean up their own messes.
- Put dirty clothes in the hamper.
- Keep shoes in the closet.
- Set out clothes to wear the next day.
- Hang up jackets and sweaters.
- Put outer wear clothes and boots where they belong.
- Keep personal body clean: bathe, brush teeth, and put on clean clothes.
- Clean bathroom after use.
- Keep bedroom clean, closets and drawers in orderly condition.
- Vacuum and dust bedroom.
- Keep shoes clean and mud free.
- Make their own school lunch.
- Keep hair clean and presentable.
- Keep brush and comb clean.
- Keep finger and toenails filed, clipped, and clean.
- Strip bed and put sheets in the wash.
- Sort soiled clothes in piles with the family wash.
- Pre-spot their own clothes.
- Put fresh sheets on their bed.

- Fold own clothes and put them away.

Family Responsibilities

Children should also begin to do family chores as soon as they are able during the preschool years, according to their age and ability, and become more involved as they grow older. The family rule should be, *"Everyone Helps." Teaching children to clean up after themselves, help with cooking, and to keep their home clean teaches children respect for mother, whose job is not to wait on everyone.* When everyone helps, mother has more quality time to spend with the family, such as reading, playing games, communicating, and family outings. She should also have time left over for herself. By learning to be responsible, children will develop pride and confidence in themselves, because they're contributing to the well-being of their home. Their feelings of "I can do this" add up.

Parents should never do for their children what they can do for themselves. Make your rules and insist your children follow them. Praise them when they perform as expected and give consequences when they don't. Remember, your child's well-being through independence should be your major goal.

I would suggest that chores be grouped according to category and written on poster board, such as bathroom, kitchen, and yard for the older kids. Each week each child would perform all the duties listed on their poster. This way they would not be in each other's way, inclined to argue and fight. A preschool child would have her own card with chores that fit her age and ability. If there's only one child, she can do a different group each week. Here are some examples of age-appropriate home chores on a school day:

A.M.

- help fix school lunches
- set table for breakfast
- clear table, put dishes in dishwasher, wipe table
- feed and water the dog
- be ready to leave for school on time

P.M.

- help with supper
- fix salad

- prepare veggies
- set table, pour milk/water in glasses
- set bread, salt and pepper, milk, ketchup, and butter on the table
- everybody scrape own plate and put in the dishwasher with utensils
- wipe table with damp cloth
- sweep floor, arrange chairs by table
- empty trash
- if there is no dishwasher, then one child washes and the other dries
- scour kitchen sink
- wipe counter top
- partially set table for breakfast the next morning

Saturdays or weekly cleaning

- wash the bathroom sink and cabinet top
- shine bathroom mirror and faucets
- clean toilet bowl, seat and wipe outside
- wipe fingerprints from doorways and cabinet doors
- vacuum carpets
- dust furniture and sills

Miscellaneous activities to be assigned when needed:

- help put groceries away
- wash veggies and fruits after shopping
- walk the dog (older kids take turns)
- see that the dog's dishes are placed in dishwasher once a week
- pull weeds in yard
- put garden tools in their proper places
- water garden or flowers
- sweep walks

Washing everyone's clothes takes mother an entire day. By the time she gathers and sorts the clothes, then washes, dries, folds, and puts them back into individual drawers and closets for her family, there's no time left to do anything else. And where are the kids when she does all this? Either playing or watching television. ***Everyone needs to do their share! If everyone helps, mother will be free to do more important things.***

School time is an exception when they have to do homework and get ready for school. However, on weekends and in the summer, they should help whenever they can.

In my family, on wash day everyone brought their own soiled clothes to the wash room, and we all sorted them together into washer loads. They each treated the spots on their own clothes and loaded the washer. I supervised loading the washer and the dryer. After washing and drying each load, we would dump the dried clothes onto the kitchen table and everyone helped fold and put them away. I color-coded the panties, shorts and socks with colored markers to determine who owned them.

Kids should also be responsible for keeping their drawers and closets in an organized state. Before my kids could go out to play on Saturday we had room inspection. Disorganized clothes or other contents in drawers were dumped on the bed to be refolded, or reorganized and placed back neatly. Closets had to be organized with shirts and trousers together on hangers and shoes in proper places. Then they were allowed to go outside to play. I can remember my nine-year-old son, Paul crying, "No, Mom. Please don't," while I dumped the contents of his messy drawers on the bed to be sorted, folded and organized properly. He was always the last to go out to play.

I had a particular problem with my kids leaving things like books, shoes, pencils, and dirty dishes laying around the house on the sofa, the front room floor, kitchen table, or wherever they were when last used. Rather than continuously nagging them to put their things away or clean up after them, I assigned each one a room to keep clean and uncluttered for a week. They also got to charge the owner of items left out of place, (which also included Mom and Dad), a quarter or dime, which was placed in the family bank. The kids were great about charging each other! Even though this caused a lot of bickering and arguing, they soon learned to put their things away, and we had a reasonably uncluttered house. And we had fun because at the end of the month we would have enough money to take the family out for pizza or ice cream.

Positive Feedback

Children need consequences, both good and bad, for their behavior. I highly stress praise and rewards for good behavior as outlined in Chapter 9, "Praise and Rewards." *Study the different ways you can give your children verbal reinforcement for good behavior and select methods of rewards you may offer them when they succeed in accomplishing more difficult behaviors.* Both are very important.

Negative Consequences

*The chores I listed sound overwhelming, but keep in mind that **you will be teaching them one at a time and over a span of several years.** Kids won't be able to do a perfect job of cleaning their bedrooms, doing schoolwork, or cleaning the bathroom, at first. But they will gradually get better with practice and age. They'll procrastinate and waste time; they'll complain, fight and argue, and if you don't keep your cool, you will find yourself nagging, shouting, and threatening (kids have a way of bringing out the worst in you). **You will need to be prepared beforehand with consequences that you previously discussed with your children, as to what the penalty will be if they break your rules, or neglect their responsibilities. And you must be consistent; if you are not, then all your time and effort will be for nothing.***

Here are some examples of behavior rules and consequences:

If you:

- are 30 minutes late going to bed, you'll have to go to bed thirty minutes early the next night.
- can't get up on time, you will have to go to bed early that same night.
- don't put your things away, then you won't get to use them for a week.
- don't do a good job, you will have to do it over.
- are disrespectful to me, you will lose your cell phone for a week
- disregard dinner table rules, you will have to eat your dinner in your room.
- lie, you will lose all privileges for a week.
- destroy something, you will have to replace it with your own money.
- steal, you will have to return the item, apologize, and make amends.
- use bad language, you will lose your cell phone privileges for a week.
- call your siblings names or hurt them, you will spend hours in your room.
- don't stop fighting when I tell you, I will make you sit still on a chair for 15 min.
- use your cell phone when its prohibited, you won't get to use it for a week.
- don't do your chores, you won't be able to play outside
- don't do your chores and someone else must do them, then you will have to pay them.

There are other behaviors that will drive you to nagging incessantly, but it won't do you any good; your kids will ignore you and keep on ignoring you until you blow your stack and your blood pressure goes up. To keep from nagging and reminding in my family, I developed a system whereby I would tell my kids to do something, such as clean up their mess and get ready for dinner, stop arguing, or get off the phone. I would begin to count to three, and if I got there and they hadn't started to obey, they would have to put a quarter in the family bank. I guarantee this to work.

If you follow my suggestions you will never be sorry. When your children are in their middle years of school they will be well on their way to independence and success; on the other hand, if you don't teach them responsibility, and demand adherence to rules, your family life will be total chaos. You will always have to wait on them and clean up after them, and they may very well grow up to be failures if they cannot be responsible for whatever happens to them. Remember this: Success comes only to responsible people. You will not be helping your children if you don't teach them to be responsible for their own personal needs and desires.

Chapter 7

BELIEF IS A SELF-FULFILLING PROPHECY

"Man is what he believes...."

Anton Chekhov

Self-Esteem is the sum of the beliefs and feelings that we have about ourselves, whether positive or negative, which shape our behavior.

Good self-esteem is the foundation of success and high achievement.

Poor self-esteem is the foundation of failure and despair.

Our level of self-esteem determines how much we like and respect ourselves, our beliefs in who we are, and how capable we are. Liking ourselves and being capable go together. The more we like ourselves, the better we are at everything we do. ***Our level of self-esteem determines everything that we are and what happens to us.*** People who have good self-esteem have desirable personalities, are generally happy and confident, have high paying jobs, and good relationships. People with poor self-esteem are just the opposite; they have difficulty interacting with others, have low paying jobs, and don't believe in their own value. Many are consumed with anger and hate; they're judgmental and critical of others, and blame everyone else for their lack of success. *Psychology of Achievement (1986) (2014) Brian Tracy.*

Parents have the most significant influence on the beliefs their children have about themselves. Children model everything they see their parents do and say, good or bad. Everything they experience in their home environment becomes ingrained within them, and the effects stay with them for the rest of their lives. This reality follows Proverbs 22:6 in the Bible, "Train up a child in the way he should go, and when he is old, he will not depart from it." In other words, children learn from the way they live, and what they learn will forever be a permanent part of their being.

Leading Causes of Poor Self-Esteem Learned from Home

- criticism from family members
- ridicule and bullying
- demeaning comments
- name calling
- expressions of anger and hate
- fighting, arguing and shouting
- lying and stealing
- use of profanity
- too little or too much discipline
- blaming others for problems and mistakes
- irresponsibility

- little expression of love
- unkindness and lack of compassion
- lack of praise and encouragement
- constant television viewing
- disorganized, messy environment
- drug or alcohol abuse
- sexual abuse

Children are programmed by their parents, older siblings, or other influential people to feel inferior or unlikable when they hear negative comments such as:

- You can't do anything right.
- Why do you make so many mistakes?
- You look a mess.
- You're such a cry baby.
- Why can't you be like your brother?
- Why don't you get better grades?
- You're not smart like your sister.
- You never do anything right.
- You're lazy.

Although building self-esteem is a lifelong process, the foundation of self-esteem is established in childhood. That foundation can do much to help or hinder a child who must deal with difficult life issues as they are encountered.

Good Self-Esteem

Contrary to many beliefs, *you cannot make your children feel lovable and capable merely by showering them with praise and compliments. Rather, it's the relationship you establish with your children... what you say to them and how you say it during your daily contact, that is the greatest factor that determines their success or failure in life. The way you treat your children will either destroy their feelings of self-worth, or start them on their way toward building a good self-esteem while they continue to grow and become who they were meant to be.*

Following are suggestions for developing a healthy relationship with your children that will contribute to their lifetime of success. As you go over them, notice that you needn't go to school to learn them, nor study them from a book. *They are simply actions and behaviors that you need to incorporate into your daily contact with your children.*

- Establish rules and responsibilities for your children to follow. Every family member should contribute to the smooth functioning of the home and have their individual responsibilities.

- Demand respect and obedience from your children and assign predetermined, fair, and firm consequences when they don't adhere to the rules. Children need discipline and rules to follow. Consequences are partners to praise and rewards.

- Treat your children with the same respect and courtesy you expect from them.

- Listen to your children. Stop what you're doing and listen when they want to talk to you. Look them in the eye and show an interest by asking questions and making comments.

- Find time to spend with each child, alone, even if you can only afford ten minutes. Maybe while doing dishes or baking, taking a walk, or a drive to the grocery store. Each child needs to be special to mother, by herself, instead of always together with other siblings.

- Be free with your expressions of love and affection. There should be lots of hugs and kisses in your family. Hugs of approval, hugs after scolding or punishment, and hugs just because you love them. Give hugs with constructive criticism, when the child is hurting, or when you are hurting. Never let a day end without a hug, and a declaration of love and pride in your child.

- Share your feelings with your children. They need to understand sadness, anger, hurt, jealousy, embarrassment, and happiness, so they can identify these feelings when they experience them.

- Value your children's opinions. When something comes up for discussion, allow them to express their opinions, and why they feel the way they do. Never laugh at their opinions or ridicule them.

- Teach your children to be assertive. Encourage them to stand up for themselves, to complain about unfair treatment, and to express their feelings. Encourage them to refuse to join their peers in inappropriate behavior, or when treating others unfairly.

- Find time to play with your children; possibly have a play night when you and your children spend time together. Little ones like to play with blocks and clay,

- and love hide and seek. Playing Monopoly, cards, or computer games with the older ones will go a long way toward developing close relationships.

- Give your children the opportunity to make suggestions. Whenever there's a decision to make, perhaps concerning a family outing, what to have for Christmas dinner, or where to place furniture. Welcome their ideas, and try to select their suggestions from time to time.

- Allow your children to make their own choices. Start out with small decisions when the child is a toddler, such as what shoes to wear, whether to eat Cheerios or Captain Crunch, to play with clay, or to color pictures. Increase the importance with age. The time will come when they must suffer consequences like the rest of us for making wrong choices.

- Allow your children to make their own age-appropriate decisions, right or wrong. Then to abide by the results and make corrections if possible. This is how they learn and gain confidence.

- Teach your children about consequences and how every action has one. Help them understand the negative consequences that are the result of wrong decisions and how learning can take place as a result.

- Let your children understand that you love them unconditionally, especially when they fail a test, make mistakes, or make wrong decisions. At times like this, what they may fear most is that you love them less because they have disappointed you. Stress that no one is perfect.

- Teach your children both gender roles. Boys need to know how to clean bathrooms, iron shirts, and cook, just as girls need to know how to use a power drill, caulk around a windowsill, and change their bicycle tires. Teach your children that it's perfectly normal for everybody to cry when happy, sad, or hurt, whether they're boys, girls, men, or women.

- Insist on positive language in your home. Don't allow profanity, or negative words such as I hate, I can't, I don't like, or I'm dumb. Don't allow anyone to criticize another person or call each other names.

- Plan fun family activities to encourage learning and interests, and family togetherness. These could include events such as visits to an art center, zoo, art shows, festivals, museums, plays, picnics, ball games, family movies, singing, or

- dancing.

- Encourage your children to support each other, to treat each other with affection, kindness and respect, to help each other when needed, such as with homework, chores, or reading together.

- Let your children attend to their own problems, such as getting in trouble in school, not getting along with their peers (within reason), or facing consequences for forgetting their homework. This advances them toward solving more complicated problems when they get older.

- Admit to being wrong and apologize, so your children will feel comfortable apologizing when they are wrong. Let them know when their behavior is offensive and apologies are necessary.

- Criticize your children constructively and kindly. Never belittle them, or call them insulting names. Especially do not compare them with each other, such as, "Your sister has a lot of friends. Why can't you make friends like she does?" or "Why can't you get good grades like your friend, Bobby does?" Destructive criticism from parents lasts a lifetime.

- Encourage a healthy interest in animals and insects. Teach empathy and compassion for   dogs, cats, frogs, tadpoles, hamsters, insects, butterflies, moths, preying mantis, lizards, birds, and all living creatures. Search the internet together for information about their care.

- Praise your children when deserved. Their entire lives are wrapped up in obeying your rules and trying to please you, then getting scolded or punished when they don't. **They need positive reinforcement just like we do. Praise goes a long way.**

We all need to be reminded now and then that no one is perfect, especially parents who are trying to do a good job raising their children. There is no job tougher, so there will be many times when you cannot be attuned to your children's needs. Just do the best you can to learn these parent/child behaviors. When you can't stretch as far as perfection demands, make allowances for yourself and keep trying. Don't beat yourself up when you know you didn't respond appropriately to your child's needs. Apologize if you were negligent, short tempered, or couldn't follow through with your promise. Your child will understand and love you all the more.

Good Character Contributes to Good Self-Esteem

A person's good character strongly correlates with good self-esteem. People who treat others with love and respect will love and respect themselves. If you hate yourself, you will hate others and won't have any friends, which will lower your self-esteem. If you like yourself, you will like others and treat them well, and they will treat you the same way. This will cause you to see yourself as a likable person, which causes your self-esteem to rise. Psychology of Achievement (1986) Brian Tracy.

Following are some of the virtues of good character that form the core of good self-esteem.   These traits follow the teachings of the Golden Rule, "Treat others as you would want others to treat you." This is an easy concept for school age children to understand when it is used as a guide for much of the good behavior you want them to assume. *Any virtue you want your children to have must already be part of your character. Acting the way you want them to be is the best training they could have, because they will imitate you and become just like you.*

- Generosity
- Compassion
- Empathy
- Tolerance
- Kindness
- Forgiveness
- Trustworthiness
- Helpfulness
- Respectfulness
- Politeness
- Integrity

Generosity is sharing one's possessions and time with friends and others who are less fortunate. It can start out with toys and cookies, and graduate to giving money, food, and time to those who are needy and to charitable organizations. Make your child aware of unfortunate people who are poor and need assistance and those whose homes were ravaged by tornados, floods, and forest fires, and how important it is for people who are better off to help these people.

Compassion is a true feeling of sympathy for those who are suffering. It is understanding the feelings of those who are sick, or have had unfortunate experiences that cause them to suffer. To be compassionate means having a strong desire to help people, or alleviate their pain.

Empathy is understanding the way other people feel in particular situations. To have this ability, a child must first be able to identify his own feelings and emotions related to being sad, angry, happy, embarrassed, or frustrated. Some examples of empathy would be to imagine the hurt feelings a disabled child may have in not being able to walk like other children, the pain one feels when she is the object of bullying, how a dog feels when left out in the cold, or a person who has no home. A good way to teach the child empathy is through actual situations he finds himself in, as well as asking him how he thinks the characters feel in stories you read together.

Tolerance is acceptance and respect for people who are different, or are of different ethnicities, religions, and cultures. Discrimination and racism almost always start in the home and in many cases last a lifetime. Parents should make their child aware of people who are different. This can easily be done while reading to the child, or watching special programs on television. Comparing the differences in people's culture, the way they dress and live, the food they eat, and the music they play will lead to acceptance and respect. Tolerance is also important when observing others who dress differently, are disabled, obese, poorly behaved, unclean, or act differently. People with these unusual traits are seen as different, but deserve to be respected like anyone else, and should never be the object of unkindness or ridicule.

Kindness is showing love towards others. It incorporates all of the other high character traits. Kindness is doing anything nice for someone without expecting to be paid back. It's very important to teach the child that unkindness is the opposite of kindness. Unkindness is physically hurting someone, saying cruel things about someone, or any act that causes others to feel badly. Kindness is also having kind thoughts about others, and a desire to make others feel good in some way.

Being Helpful means to look for ways to help someone whenever the occasion arises, beginning with doing favors for siblings and helping around the house and yard. This means doing things for parents and friends without being asked and for neighbors and people encountered during daily activities. Examples are: holding the door open for people, helping to put groceries in one's car, handing out church flyers, checking on elderly neighbors to see if they need anything, picking up discarded trash in the street in front of your house, walking the dog or the neighbors' dog, or shoveling snow from neighbors' walks. When one looks hard enough, there's always nice things to say or do for others.

Forgiveness is a very difficult concept. It entails letting go of hurt feelings someone caused you, and the resentment you feel toward that person. It's impossible to forget a hurtful encounter, but it's very important to release the resulting bad feelings and anger. Parents need to help the child be aware of forgiveness by asking for it themselves, such as "Penny, I'm so sorry I shouted at you; I was frustrated and took it out on you. Please forgive me." Penny should be encouraged to respond with, "That's o.k. Mommy," with a hug. Be certain to encourage her to ask you for forgiveness when she hurts you in some way. For example, "I feel hurt because of what you did. An apology would help me feel better." Holding a grudge is hanging on to a negative feeling, which tears down a person's own feelings. Encourage empathy toward the offensive person and substitute it with love and understanding, even if they don't ask to be forgiven.

Trustworthiness encompasses telling the truth, not cheating or stealing, following through with promises, and following rules when parents, or those in authority aren't around. Never let your child hear you lie, and never make a promise you can't keep unless you must. There should be consequences for cheating and lying. If you suspect your child of stealing, don't ignore or hide it. It doesn't mean the child is bad. Most every child will steal, at least once, but if not caught and made to return the item, he may steal again. And most children lie; those that don't are very unusual. Learning to tell the truth usually comes with consequences and maturity.

Respectfulness is honoring other people's feelings, their rights, culture and beliefs; it is thinking and acting in ways that show people you care about them, treating them with kindness, politeness, and good manners. You show people respect by valuing their opinions and listening to them without interruption. Showing respect is obeying your parents and others in authority, as well as obeying laws. By respecting others, a person increases his own self-respect.

Integrity means to do the right thing even when appreciation, recognition, or punishment are not expected. It means continuously looking for ways to make oneself better. Integrity incorporates all of the other virtues. Examples of integrity in the home may start with little things, such as bagging garbage before putting it in the trash, not putting aerosol cans or dead batteries in the trash, doing extra chores, not talking negatively about your friends or neighbors, not cheating, even if one has the opportunity, standing up for a fellow student who is being harassed by a bully, or defending a classmate when others are laughing at or ridiculing him. It means telling a cashier that she overpaid you and calling the merchant to tell him that you didn't pay a bill after he mistakenly sent you a paid statement. The best all-inclusive description of integrity is "doing the right thing." There are hundreds of right and wrong behaviors that come up in daily life that apply to high integrity. Keep an eye open for those you can use to teach your child.

Good character must be continuously worked on; it's not something one gets and keeps. Having character flaws will drag your self-esteem down. While writing this, I discovered some of my own traits that I need to concentrate on improving. I still carry a grudge against my neighbor for offending me ten years ago. I need to work on this. Now and then I find myself being critical of others, or not contributing as much to charity as I should. One can get in a rut, and not realize that they have problems with their feelings that they can change, with effort. Be open with your children and explain some of your character defects that you need to work on. Then let them see you get better.

Doing for others will not only be helping them, but will make you feel good about yourself and raise your own self-esteem. Here are many ways you can teach your children to be kind and helpful:

- Smile at everyone you meet.
- Donate toys, books and clothes to the poor.
- Donate food to the hungry.
- Take a treat or covered dish to elderly or sick neighbors.
- Take the neighbor's dog for a walk.
- Donate time to the animal shelter.
- Do an extra chore around the house without being asked.
- Visit a nursing home, and read to the elderly or distribute candy.
- Contribute baked goods to church sales.
- Take turns being lunch partners to students who sit alone.
- Compliment friends and siblings.
- Do favors for siblings and friends.
- Feed the birds and squirrels.
- Pick up trash others have carelessly dropped.
- Be a friend to a friendless student in school.
- Help another student with an assignment he doesn't understand.
- Shovel snow for neighbors.

- Open doors for others and let them go first.
- Help put groceries and other packages in cars at the shopping malls.
- Donate time at hospitals.
- Defend and befriend students who are being bullied.

Having strong character, alone, is not enough to induce high esteem.   It must be accompanied by numerous other skills related to a person's self-worth, such as responsibility, self-discipline, persistence, and confidence. A good amount of these qualities, combined with good character, will produce a person who truly loves and values himself and is capable of achieving success.

Success Leads to High Self-Esteem

Just as it is the parents' job to help their children develop high self-esteem through good character and lovability, it is also their duty to help them build upon their good self-esteem by teaching them how to perform various tasks and projects, get good grades in school, assume personal responsibility, and accountability. Developing and maintaining good self-esteem is a continuing process, requiring a lifetime of continuous effort in which the child will experience success in some areas and failure in others.

Unfortunately, a huge obstacle preventing people from achieving success is their fear of making mistakes, or they stop trying because the mistakes they've made caused them to believe that they can't perform like others, or they're not smart enough. *So much anxiety, negative feelings and failure have been created within people, because they do not understand the principle behind success, which is that it comes only to those who earn it by making mistakes and learning from them, and the more effort one puts into mastering a task, improving relationships, or personal development, the greater the results will be.*   Parents are responsible for teaching their child that mistakes are neither bad nor good. There are no perfect people; those who have the highest success are those who have made the most mistakes and learned from them.

What would it be like if everything we tried to do was easy…if we succeeded the very first time we tried? Think for a while…would we feel pride, satisfaction, or elation because we accomplished something great? Everyone would be at the same level, qualified for any job, without training or studying. We would have, and be able to do everything we desired; therefore, there wouldn't be anything to strive for. Really scary, isn't it? Thank goodness this will never happen. *Competition is one of the keys to success.*

Wise parents teach their children that only effort will get them what they want in life.

Whether it involves getting good grades, winning a dance competition, or getting a good job, success is enhanced through error. Making mistakes and correcting them brings us closer to our goal, and the more practice one puts into mastering a task or personal development, the greater the results will be. Don't deprive your child of the opportunity to grow and learn through this natural process, without the stress and fear of failure, knowing that through persistence, success is soon to follow.

Mistakes are o.k. That's how we learn.

Help your child understand that consequences, good or bad, follow every action. Negative consequences are not bad, but the result of mistakes caused by carelessness, poor judgment, poor decisions, poor choices, or not enough effort. With the right attitude and effort to get better, success will be the result. Kindly point out the negative consequences when they happen, and encourage the child to learn from his mistakes without feeling guilt about doing something bad. Here are some guidelines to follow that will help your children accept responsibility and learn from their mistakes:

- Praise your children for their ability to accept their mistakes, not make excuses.
- Don't allow your child to blame others for mistakes he has made.
- Encourage apologies and amends for mistakes that offend others.
- Praise the effort your child puts into a project, not the result.
- Emphasize that everything is hard the first time we do it, but it gets easier the more we try.
- Help your child compare herself where she is now to where she was before, and how she made herself better through trial and error.
- Help your child understand how she makes herself better each time she makes a mistake and corrects it.
- Help your child understand that persistence is the key. If she keeps practicing, she will succeed.
- Tell your child about mistakes you made, especially the careless ones. It helps to know that those you love and respect have made mistakes, too.

Without acceptance of failure as a prelude to success, a person will give up trying before she reaches achievement. She will then spend her lifetime seeing herself as not good enough; whereas, when one experiences success, over and over again, through trial and error, she will come to believe she is good and capable. Either way of believing perpetu ates itself. **The negative believer will continue to live a life of failure...the one who believes she can achieve, with effort, will go on to continued success.**

Chapter 8

THE POWER OF THE MIND

"You become what you think about most of the time.
Change Your Thinking, Change Your Life."(2003)

Brian Tracy

Positive vs. Negative Thoughts

I once took a class in auto-hypnosis and positive thinking (affirmations). The hypnotist began the session with these statements:

"Never say or think anything about yourself that you don't want to be, because that's how you will become."

" Never, ever say anything to your children that you don't want them to be, because they will become that way."

"Never let your children hear you say anything about yourself that you don't want them to become, because they will pattern themselves after you."

According to a "National Science Foundation" article published in 2005 concerning research about human thoughts, the average person has between 12,000 to 60,000 thoughts per day. Can you imagine yourself harboring that many thoughts? *It goes on to report that 80% of those thoughts are negative and 95% are exactly the same repetitive thoughts as the day before*. This is shocking! **Why are the majority of people negative thinkers instead of positive?** Although recent studies have discovered a number of variant genes that predispose people to severe negativity, they only affect about 14% of the world population. What causes the rest of us to think so negatively?

People are born mentally neutral: neither good nor bad, happy or sad, kind or cruel, selfish or generous. *These are not genetic traits; they are among the numerous other values and characteristics that are learned.* Children model their thinking patterns and behavior from everyone in their earliest environment and closest relationships, and incorporate what they see and hear into their own lives. *As parents, we have the major role of influence. If we are negative thinkers and have poor self-esteem, our children will be just like us, and their children will model their thinking patterns and behavior, and so on. This explains how we come to believe the way we do.*

Many parents cause severe and irreparable damage to the mental development of their children when they use negative statements while disciplining and correcting them. Hearing insults and put-downs repeatedly while growing up will assuredly result in a lifetime of negative beliefs like, "I'm bad." "I'm not good enough." "I'm not capable." "I'm not lovable," and may even lead to severe depression in later years. Children who are led to these negative beliefs about themselves seldom become confident, successful adults. Remember this statement, "*You are what you believe yourself to be.*" Following are many statements parents make that lead to a child's feelings of rejection and unworthiness:

- You can't do anything right.
- What's the matter with you?
- You're not good at Math.
- You're not a good reader.
- You don't listen.
- You're such a cry baby.
- Why can't you be like your brother?
- You're such a disappointment to me.
- You're lazy.
- You're a liar.
- You're fat.
- You don't want to do anything, but watch TV.
- You're a bad girl.
- You always disobey me.
- I'm going to give you away.
- I'm going to get another little boy.
- I'm ashamed of you.
- How many times do I have to tell you!
- Get away from me!
- I don't love you when you act that way.

Ignorant parents are not the only culprits when it comes to verbally abusing their children; *older children may also be offensive to their younger siblings, which in some cases may cause equal damage.* Children can be very cruel, especially when they're unchaparoned; often they will treat younger sisters and brothers unfairly and call them belittling and insulting names, such as dummy, fatty, stupid, ugly, and even physically hurt them.

Children who are raised with this abusive language and treatment will be more vulnerable in school; they'll not only be unable to develop meaningful friendships, but they will easily think badly of themselves if they don't get as good grades as their classmates, if they are not as popular, if they don't dress as nicely, or are not as good at sports. They may even be bullies or participate in bullying other students. *If using these abusive statements are part of your parenting style, even if you make them occasionally, you must stop and get counseling to learn of proper ways to raise your children.*

And if you are allowing your older children to hurt the younger ones in the same manner, you must stop them immediately and take them with you for counseling. Here are sad examples of children's negative beliefs that are the result of ignorant parenting and sibling abuse:

- I'm dumb.
- Nobody likes me.
- I'm not good enough.
- I wish I was like her (him).
- I don't have any friends
- My teacher doesn't like me.
- I hate the way I look.
- I'm fat.
- I'm ugly.
- I'm too tall.
- I never win.

Going Forward

Positive thinking is the most valuable gift parents can give their children, ***but if you are one of the 80% of people who are negative thinkers, how are you going to help your child develop into one of the 20% who are positive? You have to break the cycle that you are caught up in and change your negative behaviors that your child is probably already beginning to imitate.***

There are three steps to laying the foundation for building your child's confidence and future success:

First: You must identify your own negative thought patterns and consciously try to change them so your child doesn't imitate them. Train yourself not to make negative statements or allow negative vibes to come from you that your child can model. You may think you're not a negative thinker, but up until you read this, you probably weren't even aware of your negative thoughts and how they control what you say, how you feel, and how they affect your life and those around you. Here are some examples of the negative statements people say about themselves that their children hear and imitate:

- I'm always tired.
- I'm always late.

- I'm bored.
- I'm depressed.
- I always make the wrong choices.
- I can't remember names.
- I can't lose weight.
- I can't stop smoking.
- I hate to get up when its dark.
- I hate my job.
- I don't like my boss.
- I'm not qualified.
- Its too complicated
- I don't have enough experience.
- I'm not smart enough.
- I don't think I can do this.
- I wasn't a good student.
- I wish I finished college.
- I'm not good at Math.
- This is too hard for me.
- I'll try…
- I hope I can…
- I don't like …
- Maybe I can…
- I always lose.
- I never win anything.

The worst negative phrases you can use in front of your kids are: I can't, I don't like, I hate, it's too hard, I hope I can, and I wish I could. They carry a subconscious message of failure which your kids will certainly pick up when they hear them, as well as the negative connotations and attitudes that you use with them. For example:

If your child asks you to help her understand her Math homework, and you tell her that Math was always *too hard for you* and to ask her teacher, she will begin to believe that Math is too hard for her, too. *Instead, tell your child that she can be excellent at Math; that all she needs to do is read the directions, try hard and proofread her work. Then sit down with her and guide her to read the instructions and figure out the problems herself, then proofread her own work. Continue to reinforce this procedure with other Math assignments until she sees her improvement, which will lead her to the belief that she really is good at Math when she tries.*

Another example: If a father takes his son's new, unassembled bicycle to a handyman, because he says he *can't put it together*, his son will most likely never be good at putting things together, either. *Instead, the father should call his son to him and say, "Let's put our heads together and assemble that bicycle. Then proceed to read the instructions with his son while guiding him to assemble his own bicycle. This would be the beginning of the son's belief that he can read directions and assemble anything that comes his way during his lifetime.*

This seems trivial, but *it's important!* Think of all the things in life that need to be assembled while following directions: cell phones, treadmills, tools, children's toys, computers, microwave ovens, doorbells, doorknobs, cameras…the list goes on and on. Imagine having to get a handyman to assemble these things for you. I remember very clearly thinking "I'm not good at this." or saying to my husband, "Here, honey, I'm not good at putting things together. You do it."

Second: Once you learn how to identify your negative beliefs and words, you must learn how to use positive affirmations to counteract them, so you can improve your own self-esteem and quality of life while you help your children develop theirs.

Affirmations are short, positive statements that we consciously say to ourselves repeatedly to counteract the subconscious negative beliefs that are preventing us from having a more successful life. The harder we try, the more able we are to change ourselves and become the way we want to be.

Select one to start with. As you say it or think it to yourself you must visualize yourself being that way and repeat it often. For example, if you hate going to work each day, your affirmation could be, "I enjoy my job and feel fortunate that I have it." Concentrate on finding things about your job that you like and be aware of them as you work. Repeat the affirmation often for as long as you need to in order to reach the point of not dreading going to work. It would be helpful to make a list of things that you could like about your job and go over them every day. *You can change your attitude about your job…you could even get so good at your performance that you would quality for a higher position.*

Another great example is a student who graduates from high school with a C average, worried that she's not smart enough to go to college. *If she changes her thinking from*

"I can't" to "Yes, I can" and works diligently while visualizing herself with a graduation cap on her head, she will graduate from college with pride and a degree that will enable her to live a much better life.

There are numerous websites that fully explain affirmations and the power of the mind. If you are truly interested, look up "The Power of the Mind" taken from *The Planet of Success*, by Steve Muller, 2016 and *The Amazing Power of Your Mind*. The information in these sites will hold you spellbound and will lead you to seek other information as well. I also highly recommend that you watch the video, *The Secret*, which was produced in 2006 and can be purchased from *Amazon*. I must have watched it at least 6 times and each time I was more enthralled and enthused about how I can further change my life in ways I want to be or things I want to have. *What you learn will be extremely valuable to pass on to your children through your words and actions. If they're high school age, have them watch it with you.*

Here are examples of *adult affirmations that will give you an idea of some of the beliefs you can develop that will help you be happier in your daily life, and become better in some way.*

- I am beautiful and smart, and that's how everyone sees me.
- I love other people and forgive those who have wronged me.
- I enjoy my job and find it fulfilling.
- I trust myself to make the best decisions.
- I let go of worries that drain my energy.
- I am kind to other people.
- I am compassionate.
- I help others in any way I can.
- I will pass this college course with ease.
- I will speak with confidence when I apply for the job.
- I attract wealth and abundance.
- Every day in every way I am better and better.
- I can be anything I choose to be.

Third: Now that you know what affirmations are and how you can use your mind to make positive changes to your own life, **you are ready to lay the foundation for your children's self-esteem by helping them to believe that they are loveable and capable of achieving whatever they want in life. The rest of this chapter will be devoted to**

that goal, which can be accomplished just during your day-to-day relationship with your children.

Infancy to Kindergarten Children

You will have the greatest influence with the development of feelings and beliefs of your infant-to five-year-old child, because they will have a completely neutral mind, untarnished by negativity, and ready for you to mold. *You can instill within them the belief that they are lovable simply by hugging and kissing them, holding them on your lap, playing, dancing, and singing with them. By praising and encouraging them as they learn to crawl, walk, climb, feed themselves, dress, and communicate, they will begin to experience the feelings of confidence and capability.*

The *Affies4Kids* is a delightful series of nine affirmation videos for preschool children available on Amazon that will make your parenting task much easier, especially if you work away from home. All you would have to do is watch these videos together and then reinforce what the children learn. Notice that most of them begin with, "I Am," which is the leading statement of believing something about yourself.

- Taking Turns
- Making Smart Choices
- I Am a good Listener
- I Am Kind
- I Am dependable
- I Am Important
- I Am Helpful
- I Am Good at Sharing
- I Am Smart

School-Age Children

Affirmations for grade school children are quite different from those for adults. Children do not have the cognitive skills to be able to concentrate on a positive thought and repeat it throughout the day, nor are they capable of determining the kind of person they want to grow up to be. Here is where the parents come in.

When your child is about eight years old, begin to teach her the *positive vs. negative* concepts: "*When you think you can, you can,*" "*When you think you can't, you can't,*" and how these *thoughts will lead her to failure or success in whatever she is trying to do. Emphasize that while she's attempting to do something, if she thinks, "I can do this," coupled with trying hard and practicing, she will succeed.*

Select activities to prove your point, such as practicing shooting baskets, studying a list of sight words, or getting a good grade on a Math assignment. These are all perfect examples of the harder you try, the better you get. When she succeeds, point out that because she kept thinking "I can" and kept on trying, she was able to achieve her goal.

This is just the beginning. You will have your child for many years, during which time there will be hundreds of occasions that will come up in your daily life which you can use as examples of the "Yes I Can" concept. Make it your family motto.

The Role of Parents

The easiest and most effective way for your children to learn positive life skills is through your parenting examples. Whatever skill you want them to develop, you must first own it yourself and then let them see examples of how you act during your daily living. *Your children will imitate and absorb what they see you do, how you do things, and what you say to them and other people.* For this reason you should be continuously aware of the example you are giving them and always be willing to critically examine your own behavior. You will not be perfect, especially if you have some negative thoughts and behavior you are trying to change, so there will be times when you say the wrong things, and the behavior you display is not desirable. *Let good come from these negative examples by explaining to your children how you were wrong and let them witness you putting in an effort to change your behavior or explain how you should have acted.* If your behavior was offensive, don't hesitate to apologize. In this way, your children will understand that mistakes happen, but they need to be corrected and learned from. *They will benefit greatly by witnessing your effort to change.*

Praise Encourages Good Behavior

Be sure to give ample praise in the forms of hugs and kisses, pats on the back, smiles, nods of approval, and high five's. That's what it's all about with kids. *It's the praise and encouragement that cause them to act repeatedly in ways they know will get your approval. When they hear your praise often enough for performing the way you want them to, it will lead them to the belief that they are that way.*

"I Am" Affirmations for Children

Below are some basic beliefs that all parents want their children to have, and simple steps for helping them develop them. **Notice that each affirmation begins with the words "I AM," because they will lead to the beginning of a belief within the child that he/she is that way.**

I am lovable. Great ways to show your child she is lovable is by providing her with plenty of affection in the form of kind words, hugs, kisses and cuddling. Tell her you love her often: when she gets up in the morning, when you leave her at day care, before she leaves for school, before you tuck her in at night, after you correct or discipline her.

I am beautiful inside and out. Inner beauty comes with all of the characteristics we want our child to develop that lead to good self-esteem. When we treat others the way we want to be treated, we truly love ourselves, and others will love us. Placing emphasis on empathy and kindness, respect for others who are different, and helping others feel good about themselves is what makes our inner selves beautiful. All you need to do is continue to encourage your children's development of all of these inner beauty qualities.

I am a kind and loving sister/brother. Siblings fight a lot, but you can encourage more loving companionship when you catch them playing nicely or showing affection to each other. Shower them with praise and approval for getting along instead of fighting. Encourage them to say this affirmation while doing "crowd" hugs (all together).

I am truthful. Most children lie because they don't want to get in trouble. It may be a real challenge to get your child to tell the truth, but when she does, make sure you praise her and tell her how proud you are of her for being truthful. Some parents tell the child she won't be punished if she tells the truth. Your goal is to get your children to own up to their guilt and be willing to suffer the consequences. Your good example of admitting your mistakes and correcting them would be very helpful. My children lied until they knew they didn't have to in order to keep from getting in trouble. Good luck.

I am honest. Most children will steal, but only once or twice if you catch them and make them give back what they took that didn't belong to them. If you should see something that your child has that isn't hers, explain to her that taking something that doesn't belong to her is wrong. Then go with her to return it, and have her apologize for taking it. This is what makes the difference between a child who grows to be a thief and one who is honest.

I am compassionate. This comes with being empathetic and can be shown in so many ways. Call your child's attention to people who are suffering and who don't have the blessings that she and her family have. Compassion can be cultivated through helping others who are in need or supporting someone who is unhappy. Understanding the feelings of unpopular students and giving them special attention is a great act of compassion; even smiling at someone will cause that person to smile back and will result in a happy boost to both people.

I am respectful and accepting of people who are different from me. The easiest way to instill this characteristic is to read books that were written to cover each specific topic. They're available on both Amazon and at the library. I have four listed below, but you can find many more just by searching the Internet. Don't overlook people with differences that aren't mentioned in the books, such as street people or those who are disabled.

> It's *o.k. to be Different,* Todd Parr About individuality Gr. 1- 4
> *The Skin You Live In*, Michael Tyler, About people with all types of skin. Gr. K-4
> Whoever You Are, by Mem Fox, Different children are the same inside. Gr. 1-4
> *The Family Book,* by Todd Parr, About all different types of families Gr. Pre - 3

I am a happy person. This can very easily be encouraged through your own behavior during day-to-day living. Talk often about being happy and share reasons for your happiness. Help your child think of reasons to be happy, and how it is so much more fun to be happy, than to be sad. Wait for actual situations you are in that you can use as examples, such as a flat tire made you cancel your family's trip to the park, so remind everybody to be happy while you have your picnic in the back yard instead. The rain ruined your child's free day from school and she couldn't play outside, so remind her to be happy while playing games inside.

I am assertive and stand up for myself and others who are being mistreated. Children will adopt this trait as they witness their parents being assertive. Try to have your child with you when you have to make a phone call to complain about something or take a defective item back to a store to get your money back. Make certain you are firm, but polite. Encourage your child to object to not getting a turn, being treated unfairly, or blamed for something she didn't do.

Make certain your children understand all types of abuse, whether it's by their siblings, parents, peers, teachers, coaches, uncle or babysitter. Explain forms of sexual, verbal, and physical behavior that is unacceptable and how extremely important it is to report it immediately to their parents, teachers, or other adults in authority. There are many books available on Amazon that were written to show parents how to teach their children to recognize and report abuse.

When I look in the mirror, I like what I see. This can be a fun activity and very effective for both girls and boys. It will make your child continually aware of something that is nice and good about herself. Make it more meaningful by occasionally doing it with her and giving your own affirmations. Make a list of affirmations and tape it to the bathroom wall. This may seem trivial and unimportant, but *it's the accumulation of little likes about oneself that lead to the total self-liking person.* Coach your child to look in the mirror and say something positive while washing her hands after using the bathroom, or at the beginning of her day. *Your goal should be to teach your child that there are many good things about herself to be proud of.*

Here are a few of many examples:

- People like me.
- I help people.
- I am truthful.
- I am a good friend.
- I do my chores.
- I am responsible.
- I am loving.
- I am a good student.
- I like my hair.
- I like my nose, eyes, ears.
- I like the way I am.
- I clean my bedroom
- I like myself.
- I can do anything I want.
- I'm special.
- I'm lovable.
- I'm proud of myself.

For a delightful example of children's affirmations, show your child the video, "Jessica's Daily Affirmations" on You Tube which went viral way back in 2010. Jessica is about six years old and is standing on a bathroom cabinet giving positive affirmations about what she likes about herself and names all the people and things she likes. One of her daily claims was "I can do anything good." If you don't want your child to stand on the cabinet, leave a stool on the floor before the mirror. Perhaps you have a full-length mirror somewhere that would be better. A great way for all of us to start our day!

School Performance Affirmations

When your child enters school there will be different affirmations, such as those listed below, that you will want to instill, but *they will be much easier, because you will see their progress almost daily by his attitude or mindset*. Try not be to monotonous by asking him every day if he likes school, or if he obeyed his teacher. Some you will automatically be aware of, like getting good grades, always doing homework, and turning it in on time. You will know if he likes Math because of his grades and attitude, and if you have a daily reading session with him you will know what type of reader he is. *Keep up the encouragement and praise, and every now and then tell him how proud you are to be his mother.*

- I like school.
- I am a good student.
- I always get good grades.
- I like math and am good at it.
- I am an excellent reader.
- I correct my mistakes so I can learn from them.
- I always do my homework and turn it in on time.

Other school skill affirmations, such as those listed below, will be more difficult to help your child develop, because they must occur in school, when you aren't present to witness and follow through with praise and approval. You will have no way of knowing if he's learning these skills unless he tells you, and most of the times he will forget. With some skills he may be too shy, such as to ask questions or participate in class. You can make it easier and fun for him by offering a sticker each time he can tell you something he learned, and when he participated in class in some way.

- I learn something new every day.
- I ask questions about what I don't understand.
- I participate in class by raising my hand to ask and answer questions.

Family Positivity

Develop a **family awareness of negative statements, complaints, and behaviors** made by members, including mom and dad, and **let the children help make them affirmative.** The best time for family togetherness is during the main meal when everyone is present. If parents control the conversation and disallow children's arguing and complaining, **this occasion could be the most beneficial time of day.** Discussing positive occurrences helps the whole family stay focused on positive thoughts and behavior. Let each child take a turn in telling about something positive they experienced that day, such as making a home run at recess, being chosen to be on someone's team, showing kindness in some way, or raising one's hand to answer the teacher's question. This will help them put minor emphasis on negative things that happened to them and **stay focused on thinking and behaving positively.**

Count Your Blessings

Another excellent topic to discuss during your family meal time are your blessings. **Make it a special time, concentrating on the good things life has given your family that are not material goods or the result of money.** Let everyone contribute. See how long you can go without duplicating someone's blessing. Various blessings may be: parents, grandparents, siblings, teachers, pets, insects, flowers, friends, passing a test, finishing a project, having a good job, something nice your boss did, a friendly neighbor, good health, and on and on. Be certain to discuss reasons why each item or person mentioned is considered a blessing.

Make Doing for Others a Family Custom

One of the best ways you can increase your family's positivity is to help your children develop empathy, kindness, and compassion, and to find time to consistently help others who are less fortunate. Doing good for others makes the giver feel good, too; it has a positive effect on the givers' own outlook and attitude, thus increasing their overall well-being and self-esteem. Everyone benefits. *Even though parents are the busiest people in the world, they still need to find time to give to others. Without "Doing for Others," there will be a missing link in your children's line of success.*

Following are a number of suggestions to consider:

Donate your blood. Your children will be very impressed. Explain to them how many people need blood transfusions when they are injured. You may also have a rare blood type that would be badly needed. Let them observe the procedure. Here I must pass on to you my disabled son's kindness. In his lifetime he donated 80 pints of blood. It was just a taken-for-granted routine in his life. Whenever his normal blood supply was replenished, he would donate again.

Give pleasure to dogs confined in animal shelters waiting to be adopted. These poor animals live in small areas 24 hours a day, starved for attention and exercise. What a delightful activity this could be for the entire family. How much fun to each have a dog to take for a walk, not only for the dogs' exercise, but your own as well. You may end up adopting several. Who could resist them?

Spend time serving poor and homeless people at soup kitchens and community dinners. Many cities have soup kitchens where homeless people can go daily for a free meal as well as a banquet on Christmas and Thanksgiving. Help is always needed to prepare the meals, serve, and clean up. Even just on holidays would be a great display of love and kindness toward the poor.

Helping your elderly neighbors. If you are fortunate to have them in your neighborhood, helping them should be part of your daily lives, or whenever they need you. Elderly people who live alone are so vulnerable. There are so many things that can be done for them that takes very little time, but will bring them comfort and feelings of security. You and your children can shovel snow from their walks, walk their dog, take them covered dishes, share your garden vegetables, and simply check on them now and then to see if there's anything you can do to help them.

Visit nursing homes and bring pleasure to the elderly. Some old people in nursing homes have no one to visit them and are very lonely. You and your children can bring them pleasure by visiting them and bringing them candy, cookies, and small gifts. Some may even enjoy being read to. Encourage your children to make small gifts for them, such as cards, clay objects, and artwork. This could become a custom that your family does perhaps on the first Sunday of each month. Consider after church, if you are church goers, or after Sunday breakfast.

Charitable money-raising activities and food drives. Be involved with your children in raising money or food for charitable organizations that will distribute to the poor. You will most likely learn about these through their school or your church. Better yet, enter Charities in the Internet search bar to see lists of numerous opportunities you can become involved with.

Salvation Army donations. Always drop coins into the red kennel; in fact why not each parent consider being a volunteer with one of your older children. A good les son in empathy could be to feel how cold and tired the volunteers get while standing outside in the cold weather, and how kind it is for people to donate their time to do this selfless act.

If you follow the suggestions in this chapter, just during your daily family time together, your children will never belong to the 80% negative group; rather, they will be privileged to be part of those who make up 20% of the positive thinkers who truly love themselves and will be in control of their life's happiness and success. What's more, your family will begin a new line of positive living that will be passed down to many of your future generations.

Chapter 9

THE SHY CHILD

"You, yourself, as much as anybody in the entire universe, deserve your love and affection."

Mahatma Gandhi

Causes of Debilitating Shyness

There's nothing wrong with being shy... 40 to 50% of people say they have shy tendencies, yet *most of them outgrow their shyness, or learn to live with it with no real problems.* Shyness may be a personality trait, or it can occur in mild forms at certain stages of development in children, and will disappear when they're older. The initial causes are varied; scientists report genes that indicate some part of shyness is inherited, but *there's evidence that* **severe shyness is caused more by the way a way a person is treated by others in his home or school environment.** Here are some examples:

Poor parent/child relationships cause lifelong shyness and low self-esteem. Parents who can't be bothered with their child's feelings and thoughts, use physical punishment, put-downs, and criticisms as means of control, do more to destroy their child's self-concept than any other factor.

Criticism and ridicule by siblings or peers can have a lasting effect on the way children feel about themselves. Normal, healthy siblings will fight and argue with each other unceasingly until their parents step in and stop them. Parents should not allow their children to say hurtful things to each other, or call them disparaging names.

Being bullied and teased by other students in school has always been a problem to vulnerable children. Most children, unless they are bullies, will be victims sooner or later. Parents should expect their child to be bullied, be aware of when she is, and be prepared to help her cope with her feelings when it happens.

Being embarrassed or humiliated by teachers or coaches happens more often than one would think, and can cause the most severe form of poor self-concept and shyness, especially when the child has to deal with the same adults every day. Parents need to know their child's teachers and coaches, and be ready to approach them if there ever seems to be a problem that their child needs help with.

These behaviors toward a small child can be very traumatic to their psyche and cause inward damage that will last well into adulthood. You must make yourself aware that other people's treatment of your child may be hurting her, to the extent that her personality will be changed and she will be denied the opportunities to achieve many good things in life, because of how other people made her feel.

A shy person may:

- always be afraid of saying the wrong thing.

- have less fun than others.
- be uncomfortable around new people.
- worry about making the wrong impression on others.
- constantly worry about how she looks.
- constantly worry about making a mistake.
- never feel that he's smart enough or good enough.
- constantly be afraid of being embarrassed or looking stupid.
- see herself as too fat, too tall, too skinny, ugly, or dumb.
- be hampered in developing the self-concept and self-esteem she should have.

Symptoms of Shyness in the Toddler or Preschool Child

The onset of shyness does not appear at any definite age in children. No one can predict when they will become shy, or even if they will be shy. Symptoms may appear just when the child is beginning to associate with other children, or involved in new activities, but will then disappear as the child ages and adjusts to playing with others. Following are symptoms that you may see in your toddler or preschool child:

- afraid to be left with a baby sitter
- won't participate in day care
- is withdrawn when around other children and adults
- cries excessively when Mommy leaves
- hides his face when approached by strangers
- clings to mommy's legs when she tries to leave
- does not play well with other children

Socializing Children

Don't become alarmed if your child displays these behaviors. They may be completely normal and disappear after the child becomes accustomed to the activity or other children. But just in case, don't wait for the signs to be definite and unrelenting. You may be able to nip possible development in the bud by getting your child involved in play activities with other children. *Generally, when a preschool child is shy and having difficulty relaxing and having fun with playmates, it's because he has not been exposed enough to other children. This is especially true if the mother keeps her child home until kindergarten, and doesn't take him around other children and people.*

Children must learn their social behavior from others their own age, and will be very shy and withdrawn if they don't meet other children until they're in school. Even hav ing siblings to play with isn't sufficient. They need to be with as many different children and environments as possible, such as preschool, tumbling class, arts and crafts, day care, play groups, and different babysitters. ***Having experience with various people and environments will go far in preventing much of the onset of shyness or may prevent it altogether.***

Socializing Activities for the Toddler and Preschooler

The following play activities are the beginning of your child's socialization, which is vital to her development. ***They should be made available to all preschool children, whether they appear to be shy or not.*** These suggestions can easily be brought into your daily contact with the child and made a part of your family living:

- Expose your one-to two-year-old child to as many people as possible.
- Encourage her to smile and wave to friendly people, such as the mailman, store cashier, or neighbors.
- Don't be the only person in the life of your baby or preschooler. Leave her with other adults such as grandma, auntie, neighbors and babysitters.
- Make friends with families that have children your child can play with.
- Babysit for other parents who have children the same age.
- Teach the child how to play with others: share toys, don't push or hit, take turns.
- Introduce your preschooler to new people and children he meets.
- Send your child to a good preschool with at least a 1/10 or less teacher/student ratio.
- Enter your preschool child in tumbling, dance, or craft classes where he'll associate with other children.

Symptoms of Shyness in the School-Age Child

If you involve your child in as many social activities as possible during her preschool years, and she still exhibits some of the following behaviors when she begins school, then you can consider her shy. Shy school children:

- don't want to go to school.
- don't want to try new things.
- won't take the initiative to begin a friendship.
- are embarrassed to recite in class or to audition for a play.
- are afraid to raise their hand to answer or ask questions in class.
- are the object of bullies in school.

- are never invited to classmates' parties.
- don't want to go to parties if they are invited.
- won't participate in playground games.
- aren't active or competitive in sports and other activities

Teacher's Support

If your child is already shy, his teacher needs to know. There are a lot of ways she can help him. ***Visit with her and make her aware of your child's shyness.*** Through her encouragement she will be able to help him cope with his shyness, such as getting him to recite in front of the class, raising his hand to ask and answer questions, getting him involved in class plays, pairing him up with outgoing friends, or sending him on errands to other teachers. All of these activities will help the shy child to overcome his feelings of inadequacy. You can also depend on his teacher to tell you how your child is getting along with other students, and if he is beginning to fit in with them.

School Life

Once your child is in school, many negative things will be happening to him that will make him feel bad and over which you will have no control. For example, perhaps he's playing ball in physical education class and he makes an out and the other kids shout at him and ridicule him in disappointment. Or he may be on the little league football team and the coach chastises him in front of the other players for not playing hard enough. Your daughter may lose her best friend or be ousted from her social group. Many instances such as these will come up in the lives of children that they will have to learn how to handle themselves. ***Life is full of disappointments and failures that young people must face as they mature and continuously work to build their self-esteem. Having over-protective parents who continuously smooth things over for them won't do them any good; in fact it will keep them from learning to cope with their life's difficulties by themselves.*** However, it will help the child considerably if he has a close relationship with his parents, so he can talk about things that embarrassed him or made him feel bad. This could make all the difference in the world.

School Bullying

Once your child is in school, **you must constantly be aware of your child's social life**: who she's playing with, the games they play, who she eats lunch with, and if the other students are kind to her. ***Bullying and ridicule cause some of the worst damage to self-esteem and self-concept, and what's so sad is usually the victims don't have close*** *rapport with their parents who could help them cope and prevent damaging shyness from occurring.* Children should not have to face the taunting of bullies by themselves with no one to talk to. If your child is the object of these cruel behaviors, you need to help her overcome the hurt feelings, and help her understand that there is nothing wrong with her, just because the bullies chose her as their victim. Some schools have a "no bully" policy. If your child's school doesn't have one, see if the administration will approve one, and by all means, make the faculty aware that your child is being bullied. I would even call the bullies' parents.

The remainder of this chapter is devoted to numerous ways parents can ward off their child's shyness and promote their child's sociability.

Outgoing Activities for the School-Age Child

- Encourage your child to "Show and Tell" or give oral reports – Practice at home, first.
- Celebrate his birthday by bringing cake to his class and let him help serve it.
- Practice reading orally with a parent or friend. Emphasize expression.
- Encourage reading to a younger sibling.
- Practice reading into cell or tape recorders and play tapes for the family.
- Give your child the job of answering the phone properly and to take messages.
- Encourage your child to invite close friends to her home. Plan activities such as a visit to the park, shopping, browsing in the library.
- Enter your child in extracurricular activities he would enjoy, such as sports, 4-H, dog training, art, or voice.
- While at the grocery or hardware store, ask your child to find a clerk and ask where to find a product.
- At a restaurant, let your child give his order to the waiter.
- When at the library, encourage your child to ask the librarian to help her find books of interest.
- Let your child empty the grocery cart and pay the cashier.
- Let your child witness you taking something back that you are unhappy with.
- Let your child listen to you politely pay bills or make complaints on the phone.
- If you belong to a church, encourage your child to hand out bulletins, be involved in social events, or assist the pastor in other ways.
- Assist with community dinners sponsored by churches, or for charity.

Parent/Child Relationship

- Never label your child by saying anything that reinforces her shyness, such as she is shy, afraid, embarrasses easily, or not outgoing. She will be what you say she is.

- Don't push him into situations he may not be ready for. Pressure will cause anxiety in the child and make him worse.

- Scolding the child for being shy is the worst thing you can do to her. It will make her feel worse and lead to anxiety about other similar situations.

- Don't punish your child for not participating in a feared activity, or make her feel she is disappointing you by not being different, or not trying hard enough.

- Tell him about times when you were shy as a child and how you felt.

- Share times with your child when you were bullied in school, and how you reacted.

- Be open and relaxed talking about your feelings and about things you used to be afraid of when you were her age. Encourage your child to talk to you about her feelings.

- Over-protecting your child may cause her to be inhibited and afraid, especially of new situations.

- If other people refer to your child as shy, tell them in front of your child that he's not shy, but merely reserved, and likes to take his time before he speaks or joins in.

More Severe Aspects of Shyness in Middle School

Following are some of the more severe aspects of shyness which may appear in the older school child and continue through adulthood. If you see these traits in your child, I would strongly advise counseling, beginning with your school counselor. *Notice that all of these traits are inward…you usually won't know your child has these negative thoughts about herself. This is why it's so important to establish a close talking relationship with your child when she is much younger, so she will be able to open up and talk to you when she's having these feelings. They are not the kind that will cause her severe harm, but will be bad enough to prevent her from enjoying life to the fullest*

extent and developing a healthy self-esteem. They may even prevent her from apply-
ing for a good job, getting an education that she has potential for, or having to accept
one that will give her a lower income, because she will see herself as not being good or
capable enough.

- anxiety
- excessive self-consciousness
- constantly comparing themselves negatively to others
- continuously worried about what others think of them
- difficulty meeting people and making new friends
- preoccupation with their appearance and behavior
- spending too much quiet time in bedroom
- refusal to join shared activities
- reluctance to try anything new

***Parents are the key to preventing extreme shyness in their child, or helping her deal
with it if she is already shy.*** Understand that if your child was born with a quiet and
reserved personality, which can be a positive asset, you won't be able to change it to
one that is vibrant and outgoing, nor should you want to. The child will continue to
become the person she was intended to be, and with your guidance and support, she
will be able to develop a healthy combination of shyness, good self-esteem, and self-
confidence that will enable her to reach success in her lifetime.

Chapter 10

SOCIALIZING SKILLS

"All children are born to grow, to develop, to live, to love, and to articulate their needs and feelings for their self-protection."

Alice Miller

This chapter lays the groundwork for how to teach children social skills, emotions and empathy...all very abstract and difficult tasks to teach that won't happen overnight. They will take much time and practice, but if parents consistently teach their child during their daily contact, provide the behavior for them to model, and give continued positive reinforcement, they will be setting their children up for long-term friendships and success.

Socializing Children

In my 20 years of teaching, I have had the opportunity to observe many nine- and ten-year-old children who had difficulty making friends and being accepted by the other students. They were either shy and withdrawn, or obnoxious. Many of them didn't deserve friends; they cheated during games, they got mad and pouted when they lost, they teased the other students, they stole other's belongings, and generally displayed too aggressive behavior. *Usually, when children can't attract friends, its because their social training was neglected during their childhood. Consequently, they don't know how to behave in such a way that other children will like them, so they end up friendless and unhappy. Sadly, these children have already begun to have low self-esteem and a poor self-concept. This is the beginning of a lifetime of failure for them.*

Social skills form the foundation blocks for developing friendships. They're ways of behaving that are vital for children to learn in order to have positive interactions with others. They learn these skills through experiences with other children, modeling their parents, and instruction from their parents and teachers. Teaching these skills should begin during preschool years and continue through high school. Some skills are even learned in adulthood.

Parents can teach their children themselves or send them to preschool when they're three- to four-years-old where they're taught by qualified teachers. *These children are at a great social advantage when they begin Kindergarten, because they have spent several hours a day for several months learning how to behave and play properly with other children their same age.* Most mothers cannot possibly give their child the same amount of time and quality of training; however, they can teach a great deal during the years prior to preschool, and then continue throughout the school years.

When to Begin?

There are dozens of behaviors that we want our children to learn that will enrich their social relationships. They can't all be taught at the same time, so we must concentrate on the most important ones that are prerequisites for entering school. Important to remember is that the key to children learning these skills is much practice and continued reinforcement. Have patience and provide them with many opportunities to learn. You will have approximately two to three years to spend with your child until she goes to preschool. What you teach your child during that time will help her to be much more confident and sociable when she starts preschool and even more prepared for Kindergarten.

Importance of Praise

Always watch for behavior that you want your child to develop so you can praise and reinforce it. *Just by praising your child when he acts appropriately can help eliminate unacceptable behavior. Praise should immediately follow the behavior*, such as:

- "What a good boy you are for sharing the blocks with Kelly!"
- "I like the way you let Gabriel go first."
- "How nice of you to share your cookie with Tommy."
- While clapping your hands, "Wonderful! Look how you and Staci put the toys away!"
- "I love the way you let Patty play with your doll."
- "Time out for cookies and milk. Are you having a good time? You've been playing so nicely!"

Correcting Inappropriate Behavior

When toddlers first begin to have contact with other children, they need to be taught the proper ways to play. Children this age aren't deliberately mean or selfish...they just don't know what is right or wrong. They need to be taught that hitting, shoving, and taking things away from each other is unacceptable behavior. When my kids were toddlers they even bit and pulled hair. *Its important to chaperone them so you can teach good behavior and correct inappropriate behavior immediately, as it happens. Preschool children are usually easy to correct, especially if they receive hugs and praise when they respond.* Here are a few examples:

- "No, Billy. You cannot take the ball away from Sammy. You must first ask him if you can play with it. Let me hear you ask him. That's good! Just the way you're supposed to ask permission.!"
- "No, Billy. It's not nice to push Patty down. You hurt her. Now tell her you're sorry. That's a good boy."

- "Billy, I told you not to push Patty down. You hurt her again. Now you have to sit on my lap and can't play for awhile." Hug him when you let him off your lap and say, "Now let's see how nicely you really can play."
- "Billy, its not nice to hit Sammy. You mustn't hit anybody. Hitting hurts. Hug him and tell him you're sorry. That's a good boy." (While giving him a hug.)
- "You must not throw food, Sammy. Food is for eating. Would you like to throw a ball with Billy?"
- "Kelly, your behavior is intolerable today. You're not playing fairly and you just shoved Sammy down again. You need to spend time in your room." Hug her when its time for her to come out and say, "Now play nicely like I know you can."

As they get beyond the hitting and shoving stage, they can be left more on their own, but expect disagreements. Kids will push and shove one minute and hug and kiss the next. Be close by in order to observe and to correct hurtful behavior, if necessary, but do not intervene unless it gets serious. Otherwise, leave them alone to push and shove, cry and argue until they work things out on their own. Disagreeable behavior at this age is just the beginning, so they need to learn by trial and error how relationships work.

Kindness

Teaching children kindness will go a long way toward healthy relationships, because generally, what they give in kindness, they will get back in love and friendship. Let your children witness you emulating kindness in your day-to-day activities while you teach them to do likewise by providing them with opportunities to learn to be givers. Encourage them to give gifts to their friends, such as an extra comic book, toy car, marking pens, or Barbie Doll clothes. A great lesson in giving is letting a child select a birthday party gift and even giving a gift if she can't attend the party. *When parents practice kindness in their day-to-day family life, their children will know that they value kindness and it will become a permanent part of their character.* Acts of kindness are so important. For more ideas, refer to the list of 21 acts of kindness for both parents and children in Chapter 7, "Belief is a Self-fulfilling Prophesy."

Teaching the Child to Share

Preschoolers are automatically selfish with their belongings. Its best to begin teaching them to share at about 24 months. Begin with things like giving her part of your banana and emphasizing that you are sharing it with her. Other things may be sharing half of a popsicle, a place on the sofa, part of your cookie, your warm blanket, or even licks on an ice cream cone. Extend this concept by sharing things such as playing with her doll. Ask her if she will share it with you, and take your time changing its clothes and feeding it before you give it back to her, and thank her for sharing. Be sure you have something to share with her in return.

When the child is older you can invite other children close to the same age over to play. *Look for a mother who would like to instill the same skills within her child so you can work together. Plan ahead of time what toys he would like to play with and be willing to share with his friend.* Initially, you will need to be present so you can provide guidance with taking turns and his willingness to share, as preplanned. Don't be surprised if the children have squabbles and fight over toys, or if your child suddenly decides that he doesn't want to share his toys after all.

Using clock and sand timers are great to help the children develop patience and a willingness to wait for the timer to go off, or all of the sand to empty into the bottom half in order for it to be time to get their turn. Be sure to have treats for your child to share with his guest and perhaps a little toy you let him pick out at the dollar store to give to his friend.

Taking Turns

Every year I had 4th graders who would try to cut in front of lines to get drinks or to go out for recess, only to be met with anger from the other students and be chased to the end of the line, the penalty for not waiting their turn.

Taking turns can be difficult to teach preschoolers, because they need to learn to have patience at the same time, which doesn't come easy. The best way to begin is at home during planned play times with mother and child. Select something simple such as building a tower with blocks. Emphasize taking turns and use the words, "your turn" and "my turn" until the tower is built. Take turns selecting an outfit and dressing a doll, or running a truck around the track. Look for things within the home where the child must wait her turn, such as having to wait to brush her teeth until someone else is finished, or have to set the table because it is her turn. When you're out and about, point out to her the times you have to wait, such as in line to get a McDonald's burger or to check out books at the library. It would be so much easier if there's a sibling, because many different occasions would come up daily where they would have to take turns.

Basic "Getting to Know You" Skills

Rather than be left to eventually learn how to meet another child by themselves, children should be taught how to begin an introduction. ***Children need to be taught these basic skills and encouraged to use them at places like daycare, parties, church events, or playing at the park where there are new kids they haven't met before.*** Very likely, once you help the child look at another, smile and say, "Hi, my name is Candy, what is your name," she won't hesitate to go through the same procedure again and again each time she meets a new potential friend. You can help your child a great deal by role playing and taking turns acting the different roles. After a little practice, look for opportunities and places where you can take your child to meet other children. Here's a list of introduction skills to teach your child to ask another while smiling:

- Say, "Hi, my name is Candy."
- "What's your name?"
- Offer to shake hands.
- "What are you playing?"
- "May I play, too?"
- "Do you want to play with me?"
- "What game would you like to play?"
- "Do you come here often?"
- "I had fun."
- "Bye. I hope I see you again."

Manners and Other Social Skills

Manners can be quite easy to teach your children. ***They will copy whatever you use when speaking to them or they hear you say to others.*** Some that you don't have the opportunity to use as often will take more time to teach and reinforce. Usually, if they use good manners when they're ready to graduate from high school, you've done a good job. Below are a number of manners you will want to teach them:

- Say, "May I have," when asking for something.
- Say, "Thank you," when given something.
- Say, "You're welcome," when someone thanks you.
- Say, "No thank you," when offered something you don't want.

- Say, "Excuse me," or "Pardon me," when walking in front of someone or when you bump into them.
- Listen and then respond when others speak to you.
- Take turns while talking with someone.
- Look at the person you are talking to.
- Don't talk when someone else is talking.
- Don't interrupt someone when they're talking to you or someone else.
- Don't interrupt someone when they're on the phone.
- Don't talk about private things in public.
- When someone helps you say, "Thank you."
- When someone pays you a compliment say, "Thank you."
- Give sincere compliments to others.
- Open the door for others and let them go first.
- Hold the door open for someone who is behind you waiting to come in.
- Pick up things for people that they have dropped.
- Say, "Excuse me," when you have offended someone.
- Say, "Excuse me," when you burp.
- Cover your mouth when you burp.
- Cover your mouth with a tissue when you cough or sneeze. If you don't have a tissue, cough or sneeze into your upper sleeve, not your hands.

Understanding Feelings

Emotions are a person's inner feelings and a very normal part of human nature. Everybody has emotions. When babies gurgle and coo, they're happy; when they're screaming bloody murder, they're mad or uncomfortable; and when they're lying peacefully with a pacifier in their mouths and looking around, they're content.

As babies mature, they begin to experience the same emotions that adults have. There are numerous identified emotions, many of which are automatically learned in the course of daily living, ***most by watching and copying how parents deal with theirs.*** Basic to preschool children are anger, joy, fear, sadness, and hurt. While all feelings are normal and o.k., some negative emotions, like anxiety or sadness, can lead to health problems in adults. Anger or frustration in preschool children can result in unacceptable behavior such as to scream, cry, stomp their feet, hit, and throw things.

Children must be taught to identify their feelings and how to behave appropriately before they start school. How would it look for a 3rd grade child to burst into tears in front of her class, because she couldn't be captain of her Spelling team, or a twelve-year-old child who throws a tantrum if he misses a basket during a basketball game? Beginning in childhood, people tend to associate with those who are like-minded and have similar behaviors and interests. Children who have positive emotions and are in control of their negative feelings will attract friends who are similar in nature, which will lead to a healthy self-esteem and self-concept. Those who cannot control their negative emotions will have difficulty forming healthy social relationships, which will lead to low self-esteem and poor self-concepts.

Teaching children how to identify their emotions and to express them in acceptable words and behavior is an important step in their emotional development. ***They are easy to teach, just during your day-to-day relationship.*** Here are several very simple strategies you can follow:

1. ***Role Modeling***

   Always remember, your child will copy whatever he sees you do and hears you say. ***So if you already have acceptable behavior, good habits, and good character, much of your job will be done.***

   Make up scenarios that create emotions and act them out while explaining to your child the proper way to deal with them, or wait until you have legitimate feelings that you can share with her. Either way will work beautifully. To begin with, just select one or two feelings to work on until the child is ready to learn more. A good example of anger for a preschool child could be slamming the door, or kicking something when you're upset. An example of inappropriate behavior resulting from being happy would be jumping up and down, screaming while in front of people.

2. ***Teaching Through Personal Emotions***

   This can be done when your child is in preschool to second grade. Watch for feelings she experiences and identify them, such as: When she gets to visit Grandma, she is happy or excited. When his brother knocks down his tower of blocks, he is angry or frustrated. When he fell off his bike and skinned his knee, he was hurt. When she wasn't invited to a party, her feelings were hurt. How is the hurt different? When the neighbor's dog growled at him, he was frightened. When her friend cancelled their play date, she was sad or disappointed. When another student made fun of her shoes, she was offended or insulted.

3. *Empathy*

Having "empathy" is the ability to put one's mind into the mind of another individual and understand what that person is feeling or thinking, and then respond with a desire to help that person. Empathy is a very complex and important life skill for people to learn that will lead to positive relationships with other people. Children who develop empathy have more sincere friendships, usually do better in school, and have higher self-esteem. Older children and adults who weren't taught to understand the feelings of others are more prone to violence and aggression.

Parents can easily teach their children empathy at the same time they help them understand their own emotions just by asking them how they would feel in similar situations, or by making them up, such as,

How would you feel if:

- you didn't have a home?
- you were disabled and had to use a wheelchair?
- you had no friends in school?
- other students bullied you?
- you didn't get Valentines at a school party?
- you didn't get invited to a party that everyone else was invited to?
- you always got poor grades in school?
- you were a dog and your owner forgot to feed you?
- you were a bird or squirrel and couldn't find food in the winter?
- you lost your mother when shopping at the Mall?
- someone made fun of the way you look.
- someone said you were ugly.

Teaching Emotions With Books

Reading books to your child provides an endless source of examples of emotions and social behaviors displayed by the characters. Busy parents may have a difficult time remembering to look for occasions to teach their child emotions during their daily contact time, but if they just make a 30 minute reading session a priority before the child is tucked in (or any other time), they can teach most everything, and more, that they don't have time to during the day

When reading to your child, discuss how the characters in the story are feeling and what caused them to feel that way. Here are several types of questions to ask while reading, whenever they might be appropriate in the story you are reading:

- How does the boy feel?
- What happened to make him feel angry?
- Do you ever feel that way?
- How would you feel if that happened to you?
- How would you get over being angry?
- Is the girl happy or sad?
- Why is she sad?
- How can you tell?
- Point out facial expressions.
- What could you do to help her?

There are dozens of delightful books available on the Internet that will make it easy to teach your children how to identify and deal with their emotions as well as teaching manners, sharing, empathy, character development, and a multitude of other skills. I envy parents today. None of these were available when my children were little. Enter the following sites for a huge selection.

25 children's books that teach emotions and character building traits.

Oh So Savvy Mom

This site lists the books and describes the skill that is taught. There is a nice summary for each, and by clicking on the picture of the cover you will be taken to the order site on Amazon.

Talking With Trees

Children's picture books that teach good character traits

10 Children's Books that Promote Empathy

Important social skills starting with preschool:

Kindness
Empathy
Eye contact
Personal manners
Table manners

Giving and accepting compliments
Listening to others
Taking turns
Sharing
Recognizing the need to apologize
Not interrupting
Learning to forgive
Containing burps

Personal Emotions Children Need Help With:

Anger control
Fear
Worry
Patience
Frustration
Sadness
Hurt feelings
Disappointment

Television Programs and Videos

Some of the beneficial programs recommended for young children to watch are Dora, Sesame Street, Barney, Diego, and Wonder Pets. While viewing these programs with your child, watch for characters' experiences involving various emotions. When one comes along, put the screen on hold and discuss it. Ask the child if he ever feels that way and encourage him to tell you when he does.

Chapter 11

. . . .

PRAISE AND REWARDS

"All of us hunger for a word of praise."
Mark Twain is credited with saying,
"I can live for two months on a good compliment."

Old American News

Everyone Needs Rewards

Learning from mistakes is a concept that takes reaching adulthood to fully understand and accept. That's why parents find it very difficult to get their child to try hard, practice, and keep doing things over and over until they learn and finally accomplish desired behaviors. *The most valuable tools you can use to help motivate your children to keep trying are praise and rewards. Little ones will do most anything in order to get their parents' approval, and a hug and kiss. Older children need approval equally as well; however, when they have to start doing chores, and face more difficult school and home responsibilities, they may need more incentives.*

Some experts don't believe children should be rewarded for good behavior, or doing a good job. They feel children should do what they are supposed to do, because it's the right thing to do, not because they are going to be rewarded. They're not considering **that** *everyone needs praise and some form of rewards in order to accomplish, or learn something.* Think about it for a while…don't rewards shape most of our behavior? How many of us would work for forty hours without the promise of a paycheck, and how long would a college student study without the reward of a degree that would lead to a good job? Why would an athlete get up at 5:00 in the morning for weeks at a time to practice running, without the reward of winning a race and receiving a prized trophy? Animal trainers use praise and rewards of food to teach elephants to sit up and dogs to guard. Even insects' behavior is driven by the need for a reward of food and shelter.

So what about children? Why should they be left out? You can't expect children to behave in a certain way, because it's the right thing to do, before the child is old enough to understand *why* it's the right thing to do. *Children need rewards and praise more than any of us. When we stop to think about all of the behaviors, attitudes, and habits that we expect them to learn, it can be overwhelming to a child who receives no praise or encouragement, only commands and demands, then punishment and harsh words for not obeying.*

I'm not suggesting that mother be ready with a bowl of candy or a toy every time her preschooler does what she wants him to do, or dole out a dollar each time her older child does his chores, or completes his homework. That's bribery, and yes, it will cause children to refuse to obey unless they're offered a reward. *What I am suggesting is to reward specific behavior that the child is having a difficult time achieving, to help the child break a bad habit, or establish a new one.* Children, like everyone else, should be offered desirable rewards that will entice them to work hard and keep trying to do the right things.

Reward Guidelines

If praise and rewards are doled out with discretion, they can help the parents bridge the gap between the toddler stage, when the child is totally engrossed in immediate self-gratification, and when she is old enough to be reasoned with and ready to begin behaving in a certain way, because she understands it to be the right way. Following are some guidelines for using praise as a reward:

- **Don't praise indiscriminately.** Well-intentioned parents may overdo their compliments and rewards, making them counterproductive. If you praise the child for everything she does, she will soon get bored hearing she's great, smart, wonderful, or good. She will come to expect the praise, and when she doesn't receive it, her whole world may fall apart.

- **Over-praising becomes ineffective.** By over-praising your child for every drawing, project, athletic performance, and daily behavior, regardless of how well she performed, you will be giving her a phony impression of her abilities. This will eventually deprive her from developing the ability to judge her own work and herself, a trait mandatory for every healthy-minded adult.

- **Praise must be sincere.** Children know when you are faking praise and when it is undeserved. Be discreet when you dole it out, and always accompany your praise with a reason for liking the behavior. For example, "Kelly, I like the way you get your school clothes and books ready before you go to bed; that gives you more time to get ready for school in the morning."

- **Your praise can be in the form of interest and enthusiasm.** When praising the child's artwork or creative projects, refrain from making gushing remarks such as, "Oh what a beautiful picture you drew for Mommy! I love it! Look at the gorgeous colors you used! You're such a wonderful artist and so creative!" Your child will be producing an assembly line of pictures and artwork, but only for a short time. Do take the time to look at each one she brings you. Inquire about particular aspects and make comments such as: "What is the girl's name? What is she doing? Is this her Mommy? Her bed looks very comfortable. I like the way you colored her dress." In this manner, you are praising your child just through your interest and enthusiasm.

- **Be selective when praising your child.** For the child to sit quietly for an hour while Mother gets her hair fixed is a praiseworthy behavior for a five-year-old, but you wouldn't praise her at the same time for being good in the grocery store and for not fighting with her little brother in the car while driving home. Let your praise be special so the child will really appreciate it.

- **Personal compliments can become boring.** You can go overboard with personal compliments, especially when you find yourself complimenting the same things over and over. Look for specific behaviors or results to compliment, such as a clean bedroom, organized book shelves, or reading to a younger sibling. And while you're at it, make an issue over the effort the child put forth in order to complete a task. If your son wrote an exceptionally good book report, rather than tell him you're proud of him for getting an A+, you might compliment the report, then the effort and patience it took for him to write it. For example, "What a great report! I like the topic about dogs. You must have done a lot of research."

- *Praise must be specific.* Always accompany your praise with a reason why, such as: "Your baby brother loves you, because you play with him." "You played a great game! That's because you spent a lot of time practicing." "I'm proud of the science project you put together. Its unique. You spent a lot of time on it."

- *There are many times when giving praise is not in order.* If your child did not do a good job, or attempted a project that did not turn out right, then the last thing you should do is praise the child, and tell him he did a good job when he knows he didn't. In this case, you will make him feel worse if you just don't say anything. Strike up a conversation about the project; ask him what he thinks about it. Assure him that not everything he does will turn out the way he wanted it to, and when that happens, it's alright, and if he cares to do it over, it will most likely be much better.

- **Help your child to feel relaxed about making mistakes,** and point out the lessons he learns from them. The saying, "Everybody makes mistakes," is useless unless the person profits by correcting his mistakes. A good example is when 5th grader Gabriel doesn't study for his test and fails. The lesson to point out is that he failed because he made the mistake of not studying. If he cares about his grades, he'll study the next time. Another example: Kelly left her school books in the baseball bleachers, and the rain ruined them. She had to use her

- allowance to purchase new ones. She most likely will take better care of them the next time.

- **Praise, Love, Hugs, and Kisses** are the most effective form of rewards for most everyone, especially the preschool and early grade child. Almost every responsibility and good habit that we wish children to develop should be under the parents' supervision and assistance. But that's not possible, so watch for good behavior when you're with them. Even a nod of the head, a wink, a smile, a pat on the head, or a thumbs-up are signs of love and approval.

- **Praise and constructive criticism go together.** If criticism is accompanied by love and praise for correcting behavior, or doing something over, the child will continue to thrive. Many times he will perform a job and not do it right, or make mistakes through carelessness, and you have to correct his behavior. Sometimes you will have to give consequences for irresponsible behavior or disobedience. Make certain your criticisms are fair, kind, and to the point.

Negative Put-Downs

Parents should always use kind and fair discipline with their children and never take away love or use fear to make their child behave or perform the way they're supposed to. Negative put-downs will damage a child's self-concept and create fear within him that will last his lifetime. Here are examples of very harmful remarks some parents make to their children when they misbehave:

Preschool Children

- "You hurt Mommy's feelings."
- "You're a bad girl/boy."
- "I don't love you when you don't listen."
- "I'm going to give you away."
- "Get away from me."
- "I don't want a hug from you."
- "I'm going to go away."
- "I'm going to get another little girl/boy."

Older Children

- "You'll never amount to anything."
- "I'm disappointed in you."

- "Don't be such a big baby."
- "What a wimp you are."
- "You live like a slob."
- "What a dumb thing to do."
- "Even your little brother knows better."
- "How could you have done such a stupid thing?"
- "You can do better than this!"
- "I'm ashamed of you."

Encouragement Precedes Success

Children need continued encouragement! Be sure to give them ample hugs and praise, along with words of encouragement and appreciation. Here are some examples:

- "You can do this. I know you can. Just keep trying."
- "Yes, you can do it. Try a little harder."
- "Practice makes perfect."
- "You can figure it out."
- "Way to hang in there."
- "No, this isn't your best. You can do better."
- "Keep trying. You're getting there."
- "Expect the best of yourself. Go one step further."

Preschoolers' Behavior Deserving of Praise and Affection

Here are some behaviors parents want their preschoolers to perform that may be rewarded with praise and affection until the behavior has been learned:

- dressing and putting clothes away
- treating pets with kindness
- putting toys away
- getting ready for bed
- saying "please" and "thank you"
- obeying promptly
- playing nicely with others
- taking turns
- making their bed
- playing quietly in the house
- not interrupting while Mommy is on the phone

- helping to load the dishwasher

Examples of Verbal Praise

Praise should always be specific and should be accompanied with what the child did in order to earn it. Here are some examples of specific praise you can give at appropriate times:

- "Thank you for helping me put the groceries away. What would I do without you?"
- "I like the way you put your toys away! The room looks nice and clean now."
- "Your brother loves you because you play nicely with him."
- " How good of you to clean up the milk your sister spilled."
- "You did a good job cleaning your room. I love to come in here when it's clean."
- "You ate all of your vegetables! No wonder you're so strong and healthy."
- "Look how white your teeth are!" (while she's looking in the mirror)
- "You put the puzzle together all by yourself!"
- "I haven't had my hug today. Ummm, I love your hugs!"
- "Let's look at your school papers together."
- "You did a great job on your homework."
- "Your papers are so neat! You must be very proud of them."
- "I like the colors you used!"
- "Will you read to me for a while? I love the way you read."
- "I like your story! Why don't you tape it and send it to Grandma?"
- "You're getting much better! See, practice does make perfect."
- "Keep up the good work!"
- "It's okay to make mistakes. That's how we learn."
- "I'm proud to be your mother!"
- "Good job!"
- "Great!"
- "I Like this!"
- "Way to go!"
- "Keep up the good work!"
- "Good for you!"
- "Wow!"

More Difficult Behavior of School-Age Children

I'm not an advocate of giving children material rewards for everything they're supposed to do; however, they are very effective for helping to establish more difficult behaviors, to break undesirable habits, or to form new ones. Its more effective and fun to give sensible, appropriate rewards, rather than scolding, shouting, or doling out physical punishment. When the child is given the opportunity to see for himself that he can improve his behavior, break a bad habit, or achieve a difficult task, the result will be increased pride and a considerable boost to his confidence and self-esteem. These results will far better prepare the child for handling life's conflicts than punishment.

Here are some more difficult behaviors you may consider rewarding to help the child get started:

- doing homework consistently without being told
- bringing home corrected assignments so you'll know how he's doing
- getting ready for bed on time
- getting school things ready for the next day
- doing chores with a good attitude
- keeping drawers and closet clean and organized
- cleaning his room
- improving grades
- learning math combinations or tables

When offering material rewards, first discuss your plans with your child, and allow her to help in setting up the goals. The reward should not be immediate, nor for just one day of improvement. Rather, begin with one week of daily improvement, followed by a reward. Daily encouragement, such as a star on a calendar could be used, leading to the end of the period when the goal should be accomplished. For example, if the objective is to get the younger child in the habit of keeping her room clean and organized, offer her a star on a calendar for each day her room is in order for a week. At the end of a week, she would receive her reward, such as to stay up an hour longer on the weekend. Then extend the period to two weeks for a slightly larger reward, and further extend the period to a month for a much nicer reward.

Rewards should be given only to help the child succeed in developing desirable habits or accomplishments. They should not be given for every behavior parents wish their child to assume. When the child demonstrates the ability to perform the way she is

expected, the rewards should be discontinued and replaced with occasional hugs and kisses for being such a good kid. If she regresses to the undesirable behavior, then the parents should resort to fair and reasonable negative consequences. Below are suggested rewards for the school age child.

Suggested Rewards

- make popcorn and watch a video
- go to a movie
- bake cookies
- invite a friend for pizza
- a trip to the park
- a trip to the zoo
- a trip to the ice cream parlor
- extra time with a parent or grandparent
- stay up later on a non-school night
- a picnic with friends
- a picnic in the backyard

Rewards for Upper Grade Children

You may want to offer a larger reward for upper grade or junior high children who have large tasks to accomplish, or a bad habit to break that will take extended periods of time. For example, to improve grades, develop a good attitude for doing family chores, or being responsible for getting herself up and ready for school each morning. Here are some nice rewards for children who accomplish difficult tasks or who are good kids in general:

- dog obedience classes for the child who takes full responsibility for his pet
- special bedroom décor for the child who keeps her room clean and orderly
- dance lessons for the child who does her/his homework and chores
- sports, art classes, and other extracurricular activities for the responsible child

There should be some expectations that would not be rewarded, such as good behavior in general, treating others with respect, being honest, kind, and truthful. These behaviors should be understood to be a duty and should not be attached to a reward. Keep in mind, the major purposes for rewarding children is to make learning challenging and fun, while motivating them to put consistent effort into learning and accom plishing difficult tasks. This will lead them to an "I can do" attitude which results in confidence and higher self-esteem.

Chapter 12

GETTING READY FOR KINDERGARTEN

"Climb every mountain, Ford every stream,
Follow every rainbow, 'Til you find your dream."

– Sound of Music

Age Difference

What does *Being Ready* For kindergarten mean? There are a number of skills children should have in order to be considered ready for school learning, but in most schools the only *requirement* is age, which is to be five years old by October 1 of the same year. The children whose birthdays miss the deadline must wait until the entry date of the following year. When they are finally accepted, they are several months to a year and a half older than some of their classmates who began on time.

Parents are concerned about the age differences in kindergarten, and rightly so. *It stands to reason that children who are close to a year older will be more mature, more ready to learn, and stronger in body development, all of which will most likely place them academically in the upper half of the class.* Many younger children are able to overcome the differences, and eventually catch up to these older children, but not at some expense to their reading and writing ability, as well as self-esteem and confidence. Today, being younger is even more problematic, because kindergarten has become much more academic; some schools are teaching children to read, to add and subtract and understand basic fractions, which used to be taught in first grade. Adding to that is the fact that many parents have turned to "redshirting" their children, which is a practice of deliberately holding them back to give them the advantage of being older and more advanced. *So in reality, even though children must be five years old before they're allowed to enter kindergarten, the ages in any particular class may vary from five years to six and a half years.*

Redshirting

Parents are confused. They don't know when to enter their children. Should they send them when their child is the right age, or should they *redshirt*, like many other parents are doing? Most parents aren't qualified to determine if their child is *ready* emotionally, if she has had enough socializing with other children, or if she will be as ready for formal teaching as she should be. *Considering that if your child is a young 5-year-old, and she will be in class with a number of children who are up to a year and a half older, I would certainly consider keeping her home another year. In this way, when she does start, she will be one of the older children, and will definitely be ready to learn without the stress of trying to keep up, or knowing that others are doing better than she. But if you do wait another year, by all means enter her into a good preschool so she can socialize with other children and learn constructive skills while she's waiting.*

Retaining The Child in Kindergarten

On the other hand, you may choose to enter her at the appropriate age, and then decide if she is ready to go on to first grade after a year in kindergarten; however, I would be afraid the teacher would want to send my child on, ready or not, due to a quota she may have to fill. She can't retain too many in kindergarten for another year if she doesn't have room for them with the new students coming in, so she must send so many on to first grade. Your child may be one who is right on the border, so she would be passed on, which could perhaps place her in the bottom half of the class throughout her grade school years, not because she's not as smart as the others, but because the older students would have the advantage of being more advanced students.

In most of my fourth grade classes, the older students were usually the better students. Very seldom were younger students at the top of the class; most were average, and some were even learning behind grade level, having never caught up from being youngest and behind in kindergarten.

The Difference a Year Can Make.

Joshua was a child who was redshirted by his parents. This child was six years old when he entered kindergarten. All through his school years he was an A student; he was bigger than the other boys and better coordinated; consequently, he was a better athlete, which encouraged the coaches to select him for the more important positions on the athletic teams and in physical education classes. This in turn gave him much more practice, so he became even better than the other players and eventually was star quarterback on the football team. ***With each success he experienced, his confidence grew and his self-esteem soared.*** Unfortunately, not all children can be a year or more older than the other students. This truly causes a dilemma, no matter at what age the school sets the deadline. This is just an example of the difference a year in kindergarten can make in school success.

Skills Children Should Have to Enter Kindergarten

Besides age, there are a number of skills children should learn at home in order to be considered *ready* to be accepted into kindergarten. These skills also vary from state to state and sometimes district to district. Parents should contact their neighborhood school to find out what their child is expected to know, long before she is close to the accepted age. Some schools may expect the students to know the alphabet and numbers, so be sure you know well ahead of time. Most will be skills that children automati cally learn just during their daily home life and contact with their parents. *If parents talk a lot to their kids, frequently read to them, and spend time with them during their preschool years, they'll most likely be well-prepared for kindergarten, regardless of age, and very possibly be at the head of their class.* Here are some major skills that many schools require, regardless of where you live:

Personal Information – Parents can easily teach this information during daily contact with their child, just through repetition and time spent reading together.

1. first and last names
2. parents' names
3. home address
4. phone number
5. age and birthday
6. own sex
7. some popular nursery rhymes
8. some letters of the alphabet

Personal care – These skills will be known long before the child is old enough for kindergarten, just by being taught to take care of himself and help in caring for his home.

1. able to use the bathroom, wash hands
2. brush teeth, use a Kleenex
3. dresses self, ties shoes
4. dress in outer jacket, mittens, snow shoes
5. manipulates buttons and zippers
6. eats independently in school cafeteria
7. cleans up after self
8. takes care of belongings

Obedience/Listening – These skills should be initiated by parents during daily contact in the preschool years so that teachers can build upon them in school.

1. sits and pays attention
2. recognizes authority
3. follows directions
4. obeys rules

Fine Motor Skills – Children begin to learn these skills when they're three-to four-years-old, unless they're allowed to watch a lot of television.

1. use blunt scissors
2. manipulate crayons
3. draw pictures rather than just scribble
4. cut and paste
5. put large puzzles together
6. build with blocks

Motor skills – If they're not allowed to spend the majority of their time watching television, children will naturally begin building these skills during their toddler stage just by playing.

1. run
2. skip
3. balance
4. hop
5. walk backward
6. kick and throw a ball
7. climb stairs
8. clap hands and march

Emotional/Social – Children learn most of these skills by playing with siblings, neighborhood friends, or those they associate with in preschool. Those who have not been provided with playmates during their preschool years may have a severe acceptance problem.

1. can be away from parents several hours
2. control emotions
3. take turns and share with other students
4. enjoy playing with other students
5. address other students by name

Abstract Words – These concepts should be learned during preschool years just through daily contact and speaking with children.

front/back	under/over
big/little	tall/short

up/down	slow/fast
top/bottom	hot/cold
more/less	in/out
full/empty	open/close

Reading Readiness – If parents frequently read to their children from the time they are infants, they will know more than the following *reading readiness* skills required for Kindergarten.

1. follows story text from left to right
2. points to pictures when asked
3. can answer questions about story
4. speaks in complete sentences
5. can tell what a character is doing in story
6. can retell parts of a story in own words

Knowledge of the Alphabet

The remainder of this chapter is devoted to numerous fun ways parents can teach their child the letters of the alphabet and their sounds. Some will require sit-down instruction, while **many can be taught during daily reading sessions and normal daily contact. This is not intended to teach the child the entire alphabet, in perfect order, both upper and lower case letters. This is the job of the kindergarten teachers.** Names of letters and their sounds can easily be taught, such as the A while eating an apple, the B while eating a banana. Just one letter at a time....no others. Throughout the week, notice other names of things that begin with the same letter. Purchase commercial letters you can hang on the wall so you can emphasize their names, the way they look and their sounds. Look for the letter and listen for their sound while reading. How simple. If parents begin this practice when the child is three years old, by the time he's five, he could identify most of the alphabet letters and will easily learn their sounds when they are taught in school.

Alphabet Games and Activities

Choose the activities that are fun and easy for you to incorporate into your home life. Some may be too advanced. Keep them fun and stress free.

• Teach the child to sing the Alphabet Song with you. This will begin her awareness of the alphabet.

- Select just one letter at a time, either beginning with letter A, or others not in order. Look for letters that name easy and interesting words, such as B as in banana, baby, boy, bath, butter.
- Ask the child what letter he would like to learn. It may be the Z that spells zebra and the sound of buzz. If it interests him, go for it.
- Concentrate only on the upper case. Teach the lower case when you think she's ready.
- Have a chalk board, easel, and chalk available.
- Help her draw the letter A with chalk and have her say its name.
- Draw and name pictures of objects beginning with A, such as apple, ant, and animal.
- Purchase alphabet cards depicting colorful pictures of objects beginning with the letters.
- Make the letter with modeling clay.
- Make the letter with salt clay. Bake it and paint it. Lacquer it and hang it on the wall.
- Draw the letter very large, four to five feet, with chalk on the sidewalk. Have the child walk on the letter while saying its name.
- Draw the letter on newspaper with finger-paint.
- Bake cookies and pretzels shaped as the letter he's learning.
- Make pancakes shaped as the same letter he's learning.
- Label objects in the house that begin with the letter he's learning.
- Give him a newspaper, magazine, or junk mail and a marking pen to search for and circle the letter he's learning.
- Make an alphabet book. Use a spiral notebook or scrapbook. Cut and paste pictures from magazines and catalogs that begin with the letter he's learning.
- Make an alphabet scrapbook by filling in one page per letter with pictures cut from magazines and newspapers.
- Play name the letter. Put plastic letters in a bag, blindfold the child, and let him reach inside and take a letter out. He must guess the name of the letter by the way it feels.
- Play fish. Pick a letter from a bag. Name it and set it on the table. Keep picking letters and placing them in alphabetical order until the alphabet is complete.
- Pay grab a letter. Let him grab a letter from a pile. If he can name it, he keeps it.
- Make individual cards with the uppercase and lowercase letters. Play a matching game.

- Play flash cards with letter names. Show the letter, the child says its name.
- Play flash cards with the letter sounds. Show the letter, the child give its sound.
- Have an alphabet house hunt. Challenge your child to find an object beginning with each letter of the alphabet.
- Save labels from cans, food boxes, etc. Let the child put them in alphabetical order.
- Start a coupon card file. Let your child help you put your food coupons into an alphabetical order file and then turn it over to him to maintain.

PART II

 READING AND WRITING

Chapter 13

TEACHING WHILE READING

"You may have tangible wealth untold.
Caskets of jewels and coffers of gold.
Richer than I you can never be.
I had a mother who read to me."

Strickland Gillilan

Reading to your child is not only one of the most pleasurable, loving contacts a mother or father can have with their child, but it is also the surest way to make them excellent readers and good students.

According to a study conducted by Pamela High, M.D., April 2000, at the Rhode Island Child Development Center Hospital comparing two groups of eight months old babies, the group who were read to often had their "receptive" vocabularies (number of words they understand) increase forty per cent since babyhood, while the non-reading group increased by only sixteen per cent.

Make up your mind that other than major priorities such as eating and safety, with some exceptions, reading thirty minutes a day to your child will be a given, no matter what, even if the kids have to go to bed dirty and the dinner dishes are still on the table. If you ardently read and apply my suggestions while you read to your child, you will be teaching him far more than all of his teachers combined. This will carry over into his higher learning and adult success.

Getting Ready for the Bedtime Story

My three little ones were born within four years of each other, so they pretty much liked the same stories. Getting them ready for bed when they were preschool age was quite a chore…by the time I got them to put their toys away, bathe, put their "jammies" on and brush their teeth, many times it was past bedtime, and I could hardly wait to get them to bed, much less spend another thirty minutes reading to them. But it was worth it. The memories I have are priceless.

As they got older and more self-sufficient, I devised a plan to encourage them to get ready for bed at least a half hour before bedtime: I would first announce it was time to get ready for bed; then I would start counting to twenty very slowly. They understood that by the time I got to twenty, I would begin reading. The first one ready got to pick out the story. We read a bedtime story just about every night until the kids were twelve years old, with some exceptions when I was too tired, or some other event interfered. *Most importantly, we would not have had time to read if I let them watch television.*

Following are the skills that I have incorporated into this "Reading and Writing Section," beginning with preschool age and graduating to the upper elementary ages. Don't become overwhelmed…you already know what they are; you just need to concentrate on teaching them. It may help you to read through them before you read a story, or once a week to help you remember which ones you wish to concentrate on teaching. Before you know it, you will automatically recognize the opportunities the text provides and the relevant skills you can teach. Relax and enjoy this story time with your child, knowing that you are paving the way to his future success.

Colors
Shapes
Counting
Listening
Retelling a story
Speaking in complete sentences
Left to right, top to bottom

Understanding emotions
Manners
Social behavior
Character building

Word/sound association
Letter recognition and sounds
Sounding out words.

Vocabulary building
Abstract words
Sight words

Predicting outcomes
Recall
Sequence
Detail
Main idea
Inferences
Critical thinking
Comprehension
Fact or opinion

While reading, you need to get the child involved in the story. ***You can greatly enhance the quality of reading by teaching various concepts and by encouraging the child's*** *interaction with the story and the characters.* You can create enthusiasm and excitement just by asking questions that will stimulate her thinking. It may take a while, but *eventually the questions will easily come to you. You'll be able to devise intriguing ones from the material on nearly every page, ranging from very simple for infants and preschoolers to those that will lead the older child to analyze, compare, guess, judge, and rationalize, all critical thinking skills basic to being an excellent reader.* If you have more than one child, you can read to them together, and let them take turns answering questions. If their age span is too great, you may have to find the time to read to each one individually, or let the older child take turns with you while reading to the younger one.

Do not:

- worry about asking questions the child is not old enough to answer; just casually help her answer them yourself and then go on reading.
- let the number and type of questions I suggest intimidate you. The more you read to your child the easier the questions will come to you.
- feel that you must ask all the questions which I suggest. I have merely listed examples of the types of questions that may be asked; any of them will contribute to developing the child's comprehension.

Infancy to Approximately Age Three

Do not make the mistake of assuming your baby is too young to enjoy listening to you read to her. I remember a surprising experience with my twelve-month-old grandchild. Her mother had been reading to her since she was six months old. Bedtime, before she had her bottle, was also designated as story time. I read a simple picture book to her, showing her pictures of animals while pointing out features, such as colors, the nose on the bear, animals feet, trees, and so on. She thoroughly enjoyed looking and listening, and cried when I stopped reading to give her the bottle. If the baby will sit quietly on your lap and look at the pictures, then she's enjoying the session. *Remember, that language development begins in infancy. Babies who are spoken to and read to often will have a large comprehension vocabulary long before they are able to speak, so don't wait until they're toddlers to introduce them to books.*

While you are reading, regardless of the age of your child, concentrate *on how you sound.* Do you speak in a monotone? If your reading is flat and expressionless, your child won't enjoy the story as much and may very likely be bored. *The tone of your*

voice and the expression you use helps to determine your child's comprehension and enjoyment of the story. So learn to ham it up… make the words sound exciting! This is so important that you really should practice. Don't feel silly…your baby will love it when you moo like the cow, cry like the baby, or chug, chug like the tractor. Change the sound of your voice to imitate characters, such as the ogre in Three *Billy Goats Gruff,* make it squeaky like the mouse, or heavy and loud like the giant. Your child will love it.

Twelve months and Up

There's much to do and teach when the baby is a bit older.

- Say the names of objects, animals and people.
- Ask where objects are, such as the ball, doggie, little girl, a fence, or the sun.
- Imitate sounds of animals and objects: "bow-wow," "meow," "quack-quack," "knock-knock," "varoom."
- Ask the baby to point to the object or person such as the doggie, wagon, or little boy.
- Play pretend while looking at pictures: pretend you're smelling the flower and ask her to smell it; pretend you're grabbing a cookie, taking a pretend bite, and ask her if she wants some. Then call the doggie, and make sounds as if you were calling it. Kids love this and will pretend right along with you as soon as they catch on.

Two-to Five-Year Olds

Mother Goose Rhymes is one of the most popular first books. Little ones never tire of the rhyming stories, even after they have memorized and dramatized almost every one. ***Hearing poems read aloud is the child's introduction to the sound/letter connections. Being able to rhyme syllables helps the child to decipher unfamiliar words, thus expanding her comprehension and fluency.***

By the time she is out of the *Mother Goose* stage, you will most likely have read the poems hundreds of times, and she will know most every one by heart, bringing her closer to actual reading. Following are some ideas about how to utilize reading rhymes to the child's advantage:

- When beginning to read rhymes to the child, emphasize the rhyming words. After reading the poem several times, begin asking the child to say the rhyming

- words for you. For example:
  "To market, to market, to buy a fat pig,
  Home again, home again, jiggety _____.(jig)"

- While reading a familiar rhyme to your child, give her one of a pair of rhyming words and ask for the word that rhymes with it, such as "Ding Dong Bell." "What rhymes with Bell?" (well)

- Teach your child to say and act out rhymes, such as "Eentsy-Weentsy Spider," "Where is Thumbkin?" and "I'm a Little Teapot." Show her how to use her arm for the handle and the other one for the spout, then to bend over and pretend to pour the tea out. What fun!

- Read the rhyme to the child. Through repetition she will begin to memorize it. Let her read it with you. Ask her to recite the last line. Ask her to fill in the rhyming words. When she learns a rhyme or poem, let her recite it for aunts, uncles, and grandparents. Applaud for her.

- Play rhyme games while cooking, cleaning, or driving. Ask her what rhymes with words like rug, spoon, floor, day, or cook.

- Playfully tell her you bet you can trick her. Read a poem she knows by heart, and replace a rhyming word with one that does not fit. Tell her to stop you if she hears an incorrect word. An example would be "Humpty Dumpty sat on a wall, Humpty Dumpty had a great egg." When she stops you, clap, laugh, and praise her for being so alert.

- Engage in impromptu rhyming games. While driving, you may see a child playing with a ball. Ask what rhymes with ball. If you see a child riding a bike, ask what rhymes with bike.

- Throughout your contact time, recite or sing the rhyming songs. Occasionally pretend that you forgot a line, and ask her to help you remember.

- Say, "I'm thinking of something that rhymes with fat. It's furry and says meow," or "I'm hungry for something that rhymes with sandy. It tastes sweet."

Three-to Six-Year-Olds

- After reading the same story several times, make a deliberate mistake, and see if your child will catch you. Make a game of it.

- Take turns while reading a familiar book. You read a page, and let the child read the next page, using her own words (of course), or tell you about it.

- If your child knows the book by heart, read half a sentence and let her finish it.

- Change the name of a main character to your child's name. She'll love it!

- Keep her on her toes while you're reading by throwing in a foreign word every now and then, one that doesn't make sense. For example, when the ogre in the *Three Billy Goats Gruff* says, "Who's that tapping on my bridge?" say, "Who's that *driving* on my bridge?" This is a good way to know if she comprehends the story, or if she's paying attention.

- Always ask him what he liked or disliked about the story, or how he would change it.

- As you read, occasionally run your finger below the words to help the child develop left to right direction of the printed material. Point from the bottom of the page to the beginning of the next page.

- Alphabet books are excellent for teaching the child the letter recognition and sounds.

- Teach the child to associate the printed word with the oral word by pointing to a word every now and then and saying its name. The child needs to understand that all spoken words have a printed partner. For example, *Mommy*, when spoken reads *M-o-m-m-y*, in print. When you come to *Mommy* again, show it to her and spell it, pointing to each letter.

- Whatever you read, ask the child these five questions: Who? What? Where? When? Why? For example, while reading *The Three Little Pigs*, ask, "*Who* built his house of straw?" "From what did the second pig build his house?" "*When* did the third little pig build his house?" "*Where* did the first pig run after the wolf blew his house down?" and "*Why* couldn't the wolf blow the brick house down?"

- Before you begin reading, look at the title and raise questions about the story. For instance, in the book, *Muddy, the Absent-Minded Moose,* ask the child if she knows what a moose is. Show her the picture and call her attention to the strange horns and its hooves. Compare it to a picture of a horse. Ask questions

- such as, "I wonder what *absent-minded* means?" "Why do you suppose his name is Muddy?" "Do you think it may be because he likes to play in the mud?" Once she learns how Muddy became *absent-minded,* call your child or yourself *absent-minded* whenever either of you forgets something.

- Always question in a playful manner. Pretend that you, too, are wondering about the answer. Never act disappointed, or irritated if she cannot answer the questions. Help her, and praise her responses.

- Play *pretend* when you come to a picture of something that can be put into an acting episode. For example, if you see a toothbrush, stop and act out the whole process of brushing your teeth. Say something like, "Let's pretend to brush our teeth." Put paste on your make-believe brush and brush your teeth, complete with filling your mouth with make-believe water, and rinsing it out into a make-believe sink. Then set your brush back in the make-believe rack, and dry your mouth on the make-believe towel. Then let her do the same. You will get other ideas as you read, such as peeling and eating a banana, or pouring a glass of milk and then drinking it and so on. Do the same with nursery rhymes. Kids love pretending!

Five-to Ten-Year-Olds (some questions may be too difficult or too easy)

- Look at the pictures on the cover and read the title. Then ask her to guess what the story will be about. This will give her a purpose for reading and strengthen her comprehension.

- Talk about feelings. Ask how she thinks particular characters feel.

- Play, *How Would You Feel?* with characters in the stories, such as an insect in a flower, a worm basking in the sun, a tree towering over the forest, a puppy on a leash, or a broken toy. You will have to help the child empathize by creating conditions in which the creature or object is involved. For instance, the insect may be eating nectar, the puppy may want to play, or the toy may be broken and sad because it's unwanted.

- Ask questions that make her reason and give her own interpretation, such as, "Why did the other goslings make fun of the ugly duckling?" "How do you think the little duckling felt?" "What would you do if you were the duckling?"

- Teach counting whenever you come to several items that are the same, such as

- apples, birds, children, or trees. This will help her understand the counting concept in math when it is taught in school.

- Help the child identify circles, squares, triangles, and rectangles. Let her point them out.

- Be aware of pictures you can use to give the child visual practice in comparisons, such as tall, taller, tallest, and small, smaller, smallest. By using people and objects in the pictures, you can also teach abstract concepts, such as near, far, next to, and between. Use the lists of words in Chapter 14, "Abstract Words" to help you.

- Teach emotions such as happiness, sadness, anger, excitement, and disappointment. Look for situations that would cause the characters to feel these emotions. Ask the child to identify the situations and to relate to the feelings.

- Teach cause and effect questions, such as: "Why couldn't the children play outside?" (because it was raining).
  "Why did the puppy get out of the yard?" (the gate was left open).
  "If you were the father, would you allow the boy to get a puppy? Why or why not?"
  "Why was the little girl sad?" (she lost her doll)
  "How do you think the little boy felt when the children wouldn't let him play?"
  "What would you have done if they wouldn't let you play?"
  "How did the kitten get wet?"

Ten-to Fourteen-Year-Olds

At this age the child should be well into the critical thinking skills, yet this is when most parents let up on the one-on-one reading. The following examples of books are excellent for family reading, whether you have teenagers or children in elementary school. They provide a wonderful opportunity to work on vocabulary words, as well as comprehension, compassion, empathy, responsibility, and sadness. First, give the child the opportunity to answer your questions; then discuss them together.

The story, *Old Yeller*, by Fred Gipson, takes place in the Texas hill country. Travis, a fourteen-year-old boy, was placed in charge of protecting his mother and little brother, providing food for the family, and seeing to the family chores while his father was away.

His responsibilities were more than what most grown men have today (highly recommended reading). Following are some possible points for discussion:

- comparing the responsibilities of a fourteen-year-old boy today with the boy in the story
- the feelings the boy may have entertained when his father left
- why Travis didn't want another dog when his dog, Bell, died
- how Travis' mother showed him that she thought of him as a man
- what Travis accomplished that made him feel confident
- what bad habit the mule had
- how Travis broke the mule of this bad habit
- other ways he could have chosen to break the mule
- why the mule obeyed the father, but not Travis
- a comparison of the mule's behavior with your pet's behavior
- why your pet obeys your father or mother better than you
- what you would have done if you found out your dog was killing the neighbor's livestock
- how Travis felt when he found out he had to destroy his dog

Chapter 14

HELPING THE CHILD READ

"Children are made readers on the laps of their parents."

Emilie Buchwald

From Mother to Teacher's Aide

When your child enters school, your role will change from that of mother to teacher's aide. When she brings books home to read, sit with her, and listen to her read her assignment. Teachers want parents to listen to their child read at home. Many schools require the parents to sign a note indicating how much time they read with their child each night. Following are several suggestions to follow when helping the school-age child read her school books, as well as when you read bedtime stories together:

- Before the child begins to read the story, flip through the pages and look for words that may give her difficulty. Have her sound them out prior to reading the story, so she can read it without too much frustration.

- Ask her to make predictions throughout the story, such as what she thinks will happen next and what makes her think so?

- While reading, don't let the child struggle too long before you help her. She'll lose the meaning of the entire story, and then she won't enjoy it. If the word has more than one syllable, slowly sound out each syllable. Then have her sound the word out a few times before going on.

- Story clues are also helpful. Before you pronounce a word that she cannot read herself, show her how to use the pictures to figure it out. For example, the story is about a dog and his bone. The picture shows the dog digging a hole for his bone, and the sentence reads, "The dog is digging a hole for his bone." The child reads, "The dog is bigging a hole for his bone." Tell her to look at the picture and ask if bigging makes sense. Ask her what the picture shows the dog doing. Then ask, "Is the dog bigging or digging a hole?"

- If the child is confused with b and d, and p and q, make some large drawings of each pair and point out the differences with her. This will help immensely. Let her trace them and draw them. An easy way to point out the difference is to show her that the d and q face the same side as her left hand and the b and p the same side as her right hand.

- Sometimes it helps to tell the child to skip a word she can't sound out, then go back to it. Usually, when she goes back to it she says it correctly, because by reading ahead she has more meaning to associate with the word.

- If the word is a sight word that cannot be sounded out, just say the word for

- her. Then have her look at the word and say it several times, so she will know it.

- Be certain to praise her when she figures out a word. Keep encouraging her by telling her she's doing great, and is well on the road to becoming a good reader.

- When in a learning situation, such as reading with a parent or teacher, the child needs to have a book that is challenging. If she knows every word, then the book is too easy and she's not progressing. However, if she must struggle with every other word, then the book is too difficult. By struggling too much, she will lose confidence and motivation. This is when she begins to think that reading is too hard for her, and that she cannot learn to read.

- If the child is reading a book assigned by the teacher and you think it is too difficult, call it to her attention and ask her to test her again. Sometimes a child is placed at the wrong reading level. The teacher should appreciate your help.

Helping the Child Select His Own Books

Until the child is confident in selecting library books to read independently, you should be available to help him. Sometimes when a beginning reader selects his own books to read, the titles and pictures attract him, but the content is at a reading level that is too advanced. When the child can't read the book, he automatically begins to think he can't read and loses confidence. Imagine how you feel when trying to read a book that is *over your head.* If an adult does not intervene, and lead the student to interesting books that he is capable of reading, his ability and desire to read well may be permanently ruined.

I still get a warm feeling when I remember little Terry, one of my fourth grade students. He was reading two years below level and wanted desperately to be able to read *big books.* While in the bookmobile looking for books to check out, Terry latched onto *The Rise and Fall of the German Empire,* a four inch thick book, with an ugly dark blue cover, and no pictures. I tried my very best to talk him out of it saying, "Look, Terry, there aren't any pictures, and the print is almost too small to read. Besides, it's way too hard for you. Let me help you find another book," but he insisted to the point of having tears in his eyes. So I allowed him to check it out, on the condition that we read it together. He lost interest before I finished the first page, and resorted to books that I helped him select. If I hadn't been there to help him, the book may have ruined what little confidence he had.

The Three Word Rule When Selecting Books

When helping a child select books to read by himself, use the three-word rule: Open the book to any page, and have him read it. *If there are more than three words that he cannot read by himself, then the book is too difficult for him to read independently.* If you will be available to help him, or if you will be reading the books together, then the rule would not apply. You may help him select books that are of his interest level, yet have more challenging words that you can help him sound out and understand, so he may increase his vocabulary.

Reading to your child is about the most important way you can help him learn to read and do well in school, so you absolutely must find the time to read, read, read – thirty minutes every day. I know it is difficult. Sometimes you're too tired, you have other really important things that must be done, or you have to get things ready for work the next day. That's okay once in a while, just so excuses don't crop up every night until, before you know it, you may read just once or twice a week, if at all. Reading can be fit in at other times and by other people, but don't forget how important it is to the child to have Mom or Dad do the reading. You really can find the time if you just look for it. You must make it a priority! *Your child will be "little" for just a few years. Don't waste those precious years for less important priorities.* Following is a list of suggestions for reading opportunities and people who may become involved in reading to and with your child.

Preschool and Early Elementary School Children

- Try reading to your toddler or preschool child when she's in the bathtub. My little ones loved to spend time in the tub, so I would sit next to it and read to them, pause and show pictures, ask questions, and keep on reading. This takes the pressure away from rushing the kids through their beloved bath, so there would be time to read before their bedtime.

- Have older brothers and sisters read to their younger siblings. This is beneficial for both children.

- Enlist an older neighbor child to read to your little one for a short while when he comes home from school, or during the summer vacation. Pay him or her a few dollars an hour and some ice cream, or popcorn when finished.

- Ask the babysitter to read to your child, rather than watch television This would

- make the child look forward even more to being with the babysitter.

- Put audio books on your gift list to purchase for your child. They're great to listen to when traveling, or those few nights before bed when you have to pass up your reading session. The library should have an ample supply from which to choose. Save them for times when the kids are bored and want to be entertained.

- Prerecord some stories for those nights when you are too tired, and just want to put your child to bed. Let her listen to a taped story and follow it in the book while she's in bed, as well as to pass time when driving a long distance. This is also a great way for you to refine your own oral reading skills.

- Take books to the doctor and dentist to read while waiting.

- Let your child invite a friend over for *buddy reading*. Supply the popcorn and a surprise cache of library books. Refreshments will add to the enjoyment.

- A great habit to get into is having your child read orally to you while you're preparing dinner. This is excellent practice for the child. You'll be close by to help with words he's having difficulty with and, if you concentrate, you can ask him questions about the story.

- Another excellent practice activity is to have him read into the tape recorder. He can challenge himself to read smoothly and with expression. If he doesn't sound good, erase what he read and read it again. Encourage him to play the taped story to you after practicing.

Chapter 15

LEARNING SIGHT WORDS

"Book love is the path to the greatest, the purest, and the most perfect pleasure that God has prepared for his creatures."

Anthony Trollope (1815-1882)

This chapter consists of numerous games and activities designed to increase the reading vocabulary, comprehension, and fluency of children from preschool age all the way through elementary grades. Any of these activities would be an excellent way to spend fun time with your child. *They may require more time other than just parent/child contact; however, every word the child knows by sight while he's learning to read will contribute to his reading ability. Just select an activity that you can squeeze into your busy schedule and do the best you can.* They're even great for siblings to play together, an older child teaching a younger sibling, or a babysitter playing with the child instead of watching television. Any one can easily become a family habit. Take your time… you have several years.

The most widely used methods of teaching children to read are through Phonics and Memorization of sight words. Both must be taught together in order for the child to learn to read.

The *Phonetic Approach,* used by most reading teachers, employs using sounds of the letters of the alphabet to decode the words, *which is only effective when sounding out regular words; that is, those that follow the letter/sound pattern which children learn in school. Seventy-five percent of words used in children's books are irregular, meaning that they can't be sounded out by following the phonics rules. These words must be learned by sight. This is where memorization comes in, and when the two methods are taught together, the learning-to-read process is complete.*

Learning words by sight can be accomplished through two different methods: *Look and Say and Memorization.*

1. Look and Say Method

In this method children are taught to *recognize <u>regular words which name an object and are illustrated with pictures.</u> It can be practiced with preschool children who are not ready for phonics, and too young to be taught to memorize.* It teaches the children to look at the picture and its printed name, such as an apple, and when done often enough, they will know the word, and it becomes part of their sight word reading vocabulary. They may forget some of the words temporarily, but will quickly recognize them when reviewing them, or when learning to read through phonics.

Some say that this method is not necessary, that learning to read in school through the alphabet and decoding words is soon enough, and it may cause confusion. This is not necessarily so. Children are very smart and when offered the chance to learn to read just like the big kids in school, they will be delighted and filled with enthusiasm and cooperation. Imagine the feelings of pride and increased confidence when the child enters school and is struggling to decode words, and he comes upon those that he already learned by sight at home. His comprehension and fluency will skyrocket! Following are several ways to teach the child to learn words through the *Look and Say method*:

Repetitive Words/Three-to Six-Year-Olds One of the easiest ways to teach words by sight through the *Look and Say* method can be done while you are reading stories to your child. ***Even if you don't have time to do any of the other sight word activities, by working on this one consistently while you read to your child, you will be helping him acquire a very impressive sight word vocabulary.*** All of this can be done in just the recommended thirty minutes' time that you spend reading to your child every day. It doesn't take any more time, just a little more effort:

- Make a bookmark out of tag board about 2" wide by 6" long. Before you read the story, preview the text and look for words that are used repeatedly. For example, in the book, *Robert the Rose Horse,* by Joan Heilbroner, the word horse is used twelve times, so it would be a perfect word for him to learn.

- Print it on the card, and draw a picture that will help him identify the name; a simple stick figure will do.

- Show him the picture of the horse, and say the name while running your finger under it.

Then let him pronounce the word a few times while you point to the letters. Keep in mind that repetition is the key to a young child remembering words, and the more he sees the picture and its printed name, the greater the chance it will be locked in his memory.

- Each time you come to the word *horse* while reading, stop and let your child say it. Don't overwhelm him with too many different words. Begin with just one until you see that he knows it. Review the bookmark words each time you begin a new story.

- Look for other books that have the same words, and when you come upon them again point them out, so he can read them while seeing the picture.

- When the bookmark is filled, make a big issue of all the words he knows. Use

- it as a source of pride for him. Let him read his words to Daddy and his grandparents. Review the words often so he won't forget them.

Again, it's very important for the child to see the object's picture with its name and to concentrate on the printed word as he says it. Very soon the child will begin learning to decode words in school, and when he comes to those he learned by sight, even if he forgot them, he will quickly remember, and won't even have to sound them out. Here are fun ways you can help the child remember the words:

- Write each word and its picture on a 4" square of tagboard to use for flash cards. Flash them for him, or let him flash them himself. Give him a penny for each one he knows.

- Purchase a bulletin board from Walmart on which to pin his word cards. Attach it to an important place, such as a wall in the kitchen where everyone congregates.

- Let him read them to you as he points to them. Give him a penny for each one he knows.

- Give him a scrapbook in which to draw pictures of his words. Print the names under each picture, and have him trace over them while saying the word. Compliment his drawings, and encourage him to show them to others while reading the names.

- Have him read his flash cards to you while you're getting dinner ready, driving to the store or, waiting for the dentist.

- If there are siblings, let them play with these words together.

- Quality time learning these words can be spent with Grandma or Grandpa.

It needn't take a lot of your time to help the child learn sight words in this manner. Most activities can easily be done while you're doing a number of other things. And the child can practice the activities independently, with a little nudge from Mom. The more time he spends practicing these words and looking at the pictures, the more certain they will be engraved in his memory.

Special Interest Words/Three-to Six-Year-Olds Words of special interest to the child may be found on cereal boxes, food cans, candy wrappers, and juice cans. Get him started by asking him if there is a special word he would like to learn to read. Have a tablet in which to write the words he chooses. Print each word on a page, using color-ful marking pens, and decorate them with some sort of identifying clues, such as with the word *orange juice,* make the O extra large, color it orange, put a navel in it, and make splashy marks around the word juice. Sound the word out for him while you move your finger under it. Have him repeat it after you several times. Have him repeat the word frequently. Keep adding words for as long as you can maintain his interest. ***Challenge him to read his words to you at different times, such as when you are cook-ing, driving, waiting in a doctor's office, or just relaxing after dinner.***

Be aware of words throughout the day that may be interesting and fun to the child that can be added to his word list. Most four-year-olds can read *orange juice, Walmart, K-Mart, McDonald's, Cheerios* and *television,* because the words hold special meaning for them. Any word you can add to his list will boost his confidence and rightfully give him something to brag about. The fun he will have will spur him on to learning more. You might call his attention to related words such as *hamburger, milk,* ba*nanas, delicious, cartoons,* and *Big Bird.* And depending on how much time you have, you can also easily teach some of the sound and letters of the alphabet at the same time; for example, have the child say the word *television.* Concentrate on the letter V and the sound it makes. No child would ever forget the way the V looks and the sound it makes. The same can be done with the letter J. Have the child say juice and empha-size the sound the J makes. *If you just do this with a few letters at a time, the child will remember them and it will make learning the alphabet much easier.*

Glossary Words/School Children – Children who are being taught to read through Phonics will still benefit from the Look and Say Method. Already knowing words while coming upon them during reading increases the child's fluency and confidence. Many school readers have word glossaries in the back, listing the new words introduced in each of the stories. ***Preview each story's words with the child, prior to reading. Have her sound them out for you. Discuss their meaning. Practice reading the words sev-eral times so she will read them with ease when she reads the story.***

Required Reading Signs/Six-to Ten-Year-Olds Wherever we go, we encounter signs we must read, which give us very important instructions that warn us of danger, tell us where to go, and what to do or not do. Rather than glance at them and mentally reg-ister their meaning for your own use, ***take advantage of the opportunities to point out the words and messages to your child.*** There will be no need to write them on cards to memorize; all you have to do is point them out to your child each time you approach them, and verbally associate the words with the message. ***It won't take long for her to***

*catch on just through association, and they will be words she'll recognize before she
needs to decode them, thus adding to her confidence and reading fluency.*

- women/men
- ladies/gentlemen
- elevator
- restroom
- entrance/exit
- closed/open
- private
- fire extinguisher
- push/pull
- stairs
- baggage

Household Object Words/Six-to Ten-Year-Olds Although children this age are learning how to decode words in school, *knowing a word before having to decode it will
enhance their fluency and comprehension.* This activity will take just a few minutes of
your time, and *once you get the child started, she can learn the words independently
while you're busy doing something else.*

Cut a number of tagboard cards 2" x 10" and use thick colored markers to print the
names of all the interesting objects you see in your kitchen, such as stove, refrigerator,
cabinets, sink, table, window, curtains, and so on. Have the child look at the objects and
say their printed names. *Then, because the child is learning how to sound out words in
school, he may be able to use his decoding skills to sound these words out each time he
studies them. This is how you can combine the Look and Say approach with phonics.
The child will never have to take the time to decode these words when he comes upon
them while reading, because they will already be permanently engrained in his mind.*

This could be a great activity for siblings to do together. Let the older child place the
cards on the objects while helping the younger one learn the names. Reward them both
with a penny or nickel; the older child for each word he helps his brother or sister learn
and the younger child for learning. This would also be a great activity for a babysitter to
play with the child instead of watching television. The more sight words a child learns,
the greater her reading fluency, comprehension, confidence, and self-esteem. All it
take is a few minutes of your time.

Children have three months of summer with nothing to do except watch television and play, unless their parents intervene and plan their days for them. They could easily study these words for half an hour each day, and by the end of the summer would know dozens of words with little or no help from mother. Following are several ways learning these words can be enough fun and challenging for the child to make her forget about watching television:

- Have her go around the room, and read the words before meals or some other convenient time. This is an activity that can keep the child busy and out of your hair while you're trying to prepare dinner, write out bills, or do some other chore.

- When she learns the names of several of the kitchen objects, move on to her bedroom or another room, and label the objects in that room. You may want to color-code each room's words. For example, use a green marking pen for the kitchen words, blue for the bedroom, red for the front room, and so on.

- When she seems to know a group of words well, have some more fun by switching them around onto different objects, but do this with only a few at a time so she doesn't become overwhelmed and frustrated.

- Get her a scrapbook in which to draw pictures of her words and print the names underneath. Encourage her to go through her book often, flipping the pages and saying the words. She can do this while you're cooking, reading the paper, or doing some other task.

- Take all the cards down from their place, and play flash cards with them. Keep the ones she doesn't know separate, and concentrate on just those few. Have her look at one of the most difficult ones right before she goes to bed. She'll know it when she wakes up.

Keep in mind that if you tape the cards onto the objects, and then just leave them there for her to learn by herself without any encouragement from you, she will lose interest and forget even the ones she learned. You need to keep the activity fun for her, so she will work at it almost daily. Don't let her tire of it. When her interest begins to wane, try rejuvenating it with a star on the word card each time she says it correctly and a penny for each word she knows.

The following games may be played with vocabulary or sight words of any kind, such as the words the child is learning through **Look and Say** or household sight words. Once the child is in school and able to decode the words, the games won't be necessary; however, they may really come in handy with the **1,000 Edward Fry's Instant Sight Words** described at the end of this chapter. Some of these games would be excellent to play with parents in the evening when television is off and homework is done.

Children love to play these games when there is a reward to be won. Pennies are a great and simple reward. Begin by giving him a jar and 25 free pennies. An effective rule would be to have to give you a penny if he misses a word, and you give him a penny if he knows it. Watching his jar fill up with pennies he earned will be the greatest motivator. You can go even further by showing him how to count his pennies and replace them with nickels, dimes. and quarters, then dollars. Be sure to take him to the Dollar Store to spend them.

- Poster Lists – Put the lists of words on a poster and pin it to the wall. Let the child play teacher with a pointer. Write the words for him that he needs to study harder.

- Word Bank – When he learns a word, write it on a small l" x 2" piece of tagboard or stiff paper to put in his bank (some sort of appropriate container). Every few days, or whenever he wishes, have him empty his bank of words to review them or call them out one at a time while he places them back in the bank.

- Flash Cards – Let him keep the card of each word he knows. You keep the cards of the words he doesn't know. The one who ends up with the most cards wins the game. Give the child a chance to redeem his missed words by flashing them to him again.

- Flash Cards Variance – Place the cards face down on the table. Make a path leading to a reward. The child must pick up the card, turn it over and say the word in order to go forward. If she misses, she sets it aside and continues on the path; when finished she must say the words she missed in order to win the reward, which could be a quarter to put in her bank or a penny for each one.

- Stick Words – Print the words on Popsicle sticks, and stand them upside down in an empty juice can. The child removes a stick and recites the word. If he says it correctly, he places it into another can for finished words. If he misses, he must place it back in the beginning can. The object is to get all of the *start words* into the *finished words* can.

- <u>Word Grab</u> – Place several small folded word cards into a paper bag. Let him reach inside, pick one out and recite it. He continues to take words from the bag as long as he can continue to read them. When he misses a word, have him study it for a few minutes, look at it, say it, and use it in a sentence. Then put it back in the bag with the others to try again. When he knows all of the words, it's time to go on to learn new ones, but be sure to keep going back now and then to review the ones he already knows so he doesn't forget.

2. Memorization, the second method of teaching sight words. Some words do not name an object, such as horse or car, so they cannot be associated with a picture, nor can they be sounded out (decoded), because <u>they don't follow the phonetic sound pattern. These are called irregular or abstract words.</u> Examples of these words are: said, through, some, which, and walk. Since one cannot draw a picture of these words to help the child make an association, nor sound them out, children must memorize them so they know them instantly when they come upon them while reading. That's why they're called sight words. I call these troublemaker words, because when the reader comes upon them and can't sound them out, he has to skip them, or ask someone to say them for him, which interferes with his comprehension and fluency. Many elementary school children are poor readers, because they don't master recognition of these words until they're in junior high.

There are 1000 of these words, organized and listed in 1996 by Dr. Edward Fry, professor of education and the director of the reading center at Rutgers University. His words were combined with the Dolch sight words, and they were published together in a book titled the *Fry 1000 Instant Sight Words*. The words are ranked according to frequency and geared toward grade level; that is, the first 100 for first graders to know, the second 100 for second graders to know, and so on.

Dr. Fry's instant sight words comprise the most frequently used words in children's books, articles, newspapers, novels, and textbooks, so knowing these words instantly will enable children to read with more fluency and good comprehension, which will enable them to be better students in all their subjects.

According to Dr. Fry:

- *25 words in the English language make up approximately 1/3 of all words in published reading materials.*
- *100 words in the English language make up approximately 1/2 of all words*

- *published in reading materials.*
- *300 words in the English language make up approximately 65% of all written material.*
- *Over half of all newspaper articles, school books, children's library books, stories, and novels are written with these first 300 words, and most sentences are comprised of several of them.*

1,000 words for a child to learn may seem to be overwhelming, but broken down to just 100 words a year for each grade level is very reasonable. Your child will have several years to learn them…just 100 words for grade one, then another 100 for grade two, and so on. It would be great if you could add ten minutes to your story time (when you're not too tired) to go over them with your child. Keep it simple by learning just 2 or 3 a week. Summer vacation would also be a good time to learn each grade level before school begins.

Following are several ways to help your child learn these words. If you keep it fun and challenging, he will have no problem learning them.

- Have him study only the words he is qualified to learn. If he's in first grade and reading first grade books, study only those specified for first grade. If he begins to read second grade books in first grade, then help him learn the second grade words.

- Study one group of words at a time; if he's having difficulty, rather than have him meet with failure each time he tries to recite several words, just give him two words at a time, then go on to more. To memorize, have him look at one word, say it several times, close his eyes, picture it in his mind, and notice how it is spelled. Then visualize printing it on the ceiling or wall with his eyes closed. Do this with each word. Then have him read all five words. End the session when he's tired. Keep studying in this manner. Make flash cards with the most difficult ones. Keep removing the ones he knows easily and play with only the ones he needs to practice.

- List the more difficult words on a large poster board, and challenge him to recite as many words as he can. Make it fun by offering a penny for each word he knows. One hundred times a penny would be $1.00. This would be a good opportunity to teach him about money. When he earns five pennies, exchange them for a nickel, and so on.

- Keep a difficult word or words written down on flash cards and carry them in a Ziploc bag. Take it, or them, to the doctor's office, or anywhere you might have to wait. Go through them together. Give him a nickel for each one he learns.

- Put the cards in a stack, and time your child to see how fast he can read the words. See if he can beat his own time

No matter how busy you are, you will never regret reading and playing games with your children. Before you realize it, they will be in high school, but the memories you will have will be priceless.

Dr. Fry Instant Sight Words
First Grade 001 – 100

a, about, all, and, are, as, at, be, been, call, can, come, could, day, did, do, down, each, find, first, for, from, get, go, had, has, have, he, her, him, how, I, if, in, into, is, it, lie, long, look, made, make, many, may, more, my, no, not, now, number, of, oil, on, one, or, other, out, over, part, people, said, see, she, so, some, than, that, the, their, them, then, there, these, they, this, time, to, two, up, use, was, water, way, we, were, what, when, which, who, will, with, word, would, write, you, yours, than, was, water, who

Dr Fry Instant Sight Words
Second Grade 101 – 200

after, again, air, also, America, animal, another, answer, any, ask, away, because, before, big, boy, came, change, different, does, end, even, follow, form, found, give, good, great, hand, help, here, high, home, house, just, kind, knew, land, large, learn, letter, line, little, live, man, me, mean, men, most, mother, move, much, must, name, need, new, off, old, only, our, page, picture, place, play, point, put, read, right, round, same, say, sentence, set, should, show, small, sound, spell, still, study, such, take, tell, thing, think, three, through, too, try, turn, us, very, want, well, went, where, why, work, world, year

Dr. Fry Instant Sight Words
Third Grade 201 – 300

above, add, almost, along, always, began, begin, being, below, between, book, both, car, carry, children, city, close, country, cut, don't, earth, eat, enough, every, example, eyes, face, family, far, father, feet, few, food, four, girl, got, group, grow, hard, head, hear, high, idea, important, Indian, it's, keep, last, late, leave, left, let, life, light, list, might, mile, miss, mountains, near, never, next, night, often, once, open, own, paper, plant, real, river, run, saw, school, sea, second, seem, side, something, sometimes, song, soon, start, state, stop, story, talk, those, thought, together, took, tree, under, until, walk, watch, while, white, without, young

Dr. Fry Instant Sight Words
Fourth Grade 301 – 400

across, against, area, become, being, best, better, birds, black, certain, cold, complete, covered, cried, didn't, dog, door, draw, during, early, easy, ever, fall, farm, fast, field, figure, fire, fish, five, friends, ground, happened, heard, himself, hold, horse, hours, however, hundred, I'll, it's, king, knew, listen, low, map, make, mark, measure, money, morning, north, notice, numeral, order, passed, pattern, piece, plan, problem, product, pulled, questions, reached, red, remember, rock, room, seen, several, ship, short, shot, since, sing, slowly, south, space, stand, sun, sure, table, today, told, top, toward, town, travel, true unit, upon, usually, voice, vowel, war, waves, whole, wood, your

Dr. Fry Instant Sight Words
Fifth Grade 401 – 500

able, ago, am, among, ball, base, became, behind, boat, box, bring, brought, building, built, cannot, carefully, check, circle, class, clear, common, contain, correct, course, dark, decided, deep, done, dry, English, equation, explain, fact, feel, filled, fine, finally, fly, force, front, full, game, gave, govern, green, half, heat, heavy, hot, inches, include, inside, island, known, language, less, machine, material, minutes, note, nothing, noun, object, ocean, oh, pair, person, plane, power, produce, quickly, ran, rest, road, round, rule, scientists, shape, shown, six, size, special, stars, stay, stood, street, strong, surface, system, ten, though, thousands, understand, verb, wait, warm, week, wheel, yes, yet

Dr. Fry Instant Sight Words
Sixth Grade 501 – 600

anything, arms, beautiful, believe, beside, bill, blue, brother, can't, cause, cells, center, clothes, dance, describe, difference, directions, discover, distance, divided, drive, drop, develop, east, edge, eggs, energy, Europe, exercise, farmers, felt, finished, flowers, forest, general, glass, gone, happy, heart, held, instrument, interest, job, kept, lay, legs, length, love, main, matter, meet, members, million, mind, months, moon, paint, paragraph, past, perhaps, picked, ,present, probably, race, rain, raised, ready, reason, record, region, represent, return, root, sat, shall, sign, simple, sit, sky, soft, square, store, subject, suddenly, sum, summer, syllables, teacher, test, third, train, wall, weather, whether, wide, wild, window, winter, wish, written

Dr. Fry Instant Sight Words
Seventh Grade 601 – 700

act, Africa, age, already, although, amount, angle, appear, baby, bear, beat, bed, bottom, bright, broken, build, buy, care, case, cat, century, consonant, copy, couldn't, count, cross, dictionary, died, dress, either, everyone, everything, exactly, factors, fight, fingers, floor, fraction, free, French, gold, hair, hill, hole, hope, ice, instead, iron, jumped, killed, lake, laughed, lead, let's, lot, melody, metal, method, middle, milk, moment, nation, natural, outside, per, phrase, poor, possible, pounds, pushed, quiet, quite, remain, result, ride, rolled, sail, scale, section, sleep, smiled, snow, soil, solve, someone, son, speak, speed, spring, stone, surprise, tall, temperature, themselves, tiny, trip, type, village, within, wonder

Dr. Fry Instant Sight Words
8th Grade 701 – 800

alone, art, bad, bank, bit, break, brown, burning, business, captain, catch, caught, cents, child, choose, clean, climbed, cloud, coast, continued, control, cool, cost, decimal, desert, design, direct, drawing, ears, east, else, engine, England, equal, experiment, express, feeling, fell, flow, foot, garden, gas, glass, God, grew, history, human, hunting, increase, information, itself, joined, key, lady, law, least, lost, maybe, mouth, party, pay, period, plains, please, practice, president, received, report, ring, rise, row, save, seeds, sent, separate, serve, shouted, single, skin, statement, stick, straight, strange, students, suppose, symbols, team, touch, trouble, uncle, valley, visit, wear, whose, wire, woman, wrote, yard, you're, yourself

Dr. Fry Instant Sight Words
Ninth Grade 801 - 900

addition, army, bell, belong, block, blood, blow, board, bones, branches, cattle, chief, compare, compound, consider, cook, corner, crops, crowd, current, doctor, dollars, eight, electric, elements, enjoy, entered, except, exciting, expect, famous, fit, flat, fruit, fun, guess, hat, hit, indicate, industry, insects, interesting, Japanese, lie, lifted, loud, major, mall, meat, mine, modern, movement, necessary, observe, park, particular, planets, poem, pole, position, process, property, provide, rather, rhythm, rich, safe, sand, science, sell, send, sense, seven, sharp, shoulder, sight, silent, soldiers, spot, spread, stream, string, suggested, supply, swim, terms, thick, thin, thus, tied, tone, trade, tube, value, wash, wasn't, weight, wife, wings, won't

Dr. Fry Instant Sight Words
Tenth Grade 901 - 1000

action, actually, adjective, afraid, agreed, ahead, allow, apple, arrived, born, bought, British, capital, chance, chart, church, column, company, conditions, corn, cotton, cows, create, dead, deal, death, details, determine, difficult, division, doesn't, effect, entire, especially, evening, experience, factories, fair, fear, fig, forward, France, fresh, Greek, gun, hoe, huge, isn't, led, level, located, march, match, molecules, northern, nose, office, opposite, oxygen, plural, prepared, pretty, printed, radio, repeated, rope, rose, score, seat, settled, shoes, shop, similar, sir, sister, smell, solution, southern, steel, stretched, substances, suffix, sugar, tools, total, track, triangle, truck, underline, various, view, Washington, we'll, western, win, women, workers, wouldn't, wrong, yellow

Chapter 16

···

ABSTRACT WORDS

"Seek not to understand that you may believe,

But believe that you may understand."

Saint Augustine

Opposites

The following words are called "abstract" words because they do not name objects. *Many beginning readers can read the words, but have difficulty understanding their meanings.* Left on their own with just the normal family communication, children eventually learn the meanings, but many cause confusion until the children reach the middle years of school. This affects their reading comprehension. *These are easy to teach and can be a lot of fun for the family.* You can begin teaching the easier ones to toddlers as soon as they begin talking. *Some are simple enough to teach while at the kitchen table or lounging in the front room. If you keep a list of these words with the child's bedtime story book you can easily teach most of them while reading to him.*

in	out	over	under
left	right	front	back
here	there	hot	cold
under	over	above	below
up	down	back	front
outside	inside	near	far
middle	end	forward	backward
open	close	alongside	between
yonder	near	beyond	beneath
middle	end	first	last
bitter	sweet	tall	short

- First print the words on poster board, so you can keep track of them. Use them in your daily contact with the child.

- Select one word at a time and use it in your normal day-to-day conversation. Go into more detail to explain the concept when you first use it. Each word should be used several times in different situations.

- Select one or two words and create your own opportunities to explain the meanings.

- A convenient time to teach the words is while you are reading to the child. Look for pictures you can use for examples of positions of objects and characters, such as a child standing alongside a house, a dog sitting between a child and his mother, a balloon hovering above a table, or a cat beneath a chair.

- It might be helpful to write the words you want to teach your child on a book-mark to keep in the book you are reading to him.

- An enjoyable learning period can be played with blocks. Ask her to bring a block here (to you), then take one and leave it there (on the end table). Put a block in the box, then take it out of the box. Put a red block between or in the middle of two green blocks. Put a green block next to or beside a blue one, put the red one on top of the green one, and so on.

- You may also make an obstacle course with pillows, sofa cushions, a footstool, and cardboard boxes. Make a list of the words you can use, telling the child where to go: crawl across or over the pillows, through the tunnel made with boxes and over the stool; stand next to the cushion, sit beside the box, and so on. What great fun! And once the child begins to read, you can use the same lists to teach her to recognize the words by sight.

- Take your child into the yard and look for objects to walk around, stand next to, beside or behind. Stand to the left side of the tree and then move over to the right side.

- Jump across the hose and have your child follow you. Then have her walk around the tree, stand between you and the tree, in front of the tree, and behind it.

You'll be surprised at how quickly your child will catch on to the meanings of these words with just a little bit of concentrated effort on your part.

Words Ending in er and est

These words are not abstract, but are still difficult for some children to comprehend. *They're very simple to teach* and knowing them will help the child's comprehension considerably. Here are just a few of the easiest ones to explain through everyday experiences.

big	bigger	biggest
hot	hotter	hottest
thin	thinner	thinnest
short	shorter	shortest
flat	flatter	flattest
cold	colder	coldest

sweet	sweeter	sweetest
small	smaller	smallest
thick	thicker	thickest

To teach these to your child, all you need to remember is to take advantage of objects, people, or situations that you may use as examples. Then point them out to your child. For example your daughter, Mary, is playing with two friends. Ask if anyone knows who is the tallest. Then line them up according to size and say, "Look, Kelly is tall, but Jennie is taller." Point out the difference in height between the two of them. Then say, "But Amanda is the tallest because she is taller than both Mary and Kelly." Line them up in front of a mirror so they may see the differences. This exercise will also work with objects such as dolls, trucks, rocks or stuffed animals. ***Look for examples to use while reading to your child.***

Kitchen Table Practice

In addition to the er and est words, some words used in Math that cause considerable confusion to some children are the *position concepts:*

> before
> after
> in front of
> in the middle
> in between
> next to

These can easily be taught in just a few sessions with three different size objects the child can manipulate, right at the kitchen table. The objects could be a number of things: buttons, coins, rocks, or game pieces. These concepts can be mind boggling. You will help your child considerably in Math just by introducing and practicing these positions with her:

- Put the coins in order of size from the smallest to the largest.
- Which coin is in the middle?
- Put the largest coin before the smallest coin.
- Place the smallest coin in front of the largest coin.
- Put the smallest coin after the largest coin.
- Place the largest coin between the other coins.
- Place the smallest coin next to the largest coin.

- Put the smallest coin in the middle of the larger coins.
- Place the coins in order beginning with the biggest and ending with the smallest.

Here are the "shape" concepts. ***Again, you need to develop a mind-set to look for objects around you to which you may refer so you can teach your child the names of the shapes.*** If you can't find objects, make them out of paper, or even clay. They're listed as follows.

circle – ball
square – cube
triangle – diamond
cylinder – soup can
rectangle- toaster
cone – ice cream cone
octagon – stop sign

Fun ways to teach the words to your child:

- Just in your kitchen, alone, you will find most of them. For example: toaster/rectangle, dinner plate/circle, soup can/cylinder, ice cream cone/cone, and cube/sugar cube, or square. Make a stop sign for octagon.

- Look for shapes in newspapers, catalogs, and in stories as you read together.

- Draw and color pictures of them.

- Make each out of stiff paper so you can show them to your child like flash cards, or let her go around the house and match them to objects.

- Look for them while reading together.

The words listed in this chapter are confusing to most small children who are left alone to learn them on their own; however, parents can very easily teach their concepts just through their normal day-to-day contact whenever an opportunity arises, or they can make them up. Or they can be learned in just a few fun sessions, perhaps instead of playing cards or Monopoly. Imagine how much you can teach your child at the kitchen table with several different sized rocks. A little bit of effort on the parents' part will go far toward increasing the child's reading and comprehension abilities.

Chapter 17

READING COMPREHENSION

"Observing and understanding are two different things."

Mary E. Pearson, The Miles Between

There's more to reading than decoding words. *Many students learn to sound out words quite fluently by the age of ten, but they don't understand the meaning of the text. With some, this problem extends even into high school. When the child is too intent on sounding out the words and trying to relate the letters to the rules, he forgets to concentrate on what the story is about.* A common concern of teachers is, "He can read the words, but he doesn't know what he is reading." *The most important and effective way children can be helped to comprehend what they read is through one-on-one instruction.*

This is not a simple process; it involves mastery of a combination of skills which takes several years to accomplish. When the teacher has twenty to thirty students in her classroom, it's very difficult to give them all the individual attention they need. Here is where parents' help is invaluable. They can help their child considerably by reading to and with him, by talking to him, and by encouraging him to discuss his own feelings and experiences. This needn't be that difficult. Conversations can take place during breakfast, while driving, while eating dinner, cleaning up the kitchen after dinner, or shopping, and much can be taught during nightly bedtime reading. Some of the suggestions in this chapter are repetitious of what has been described in previous chapters on "Home Environment," "Language," "Sight Words," and "Vocabulary:" however it will be beneficial to go over them again. There are a lot of new suggestions as well.

Comprehension Skills

Decoding

This skill is taught extensively in elementary school. It's the first formal step to learning to read. Decoding begins even before school age when parents teach the child the letters and sounds of the alphabet at home.

- While listening to the child read, help him sound out the letters of the words he has difficulty reading.

- Keep showing him how to sound out words as you read to him, and when he begins to read himself. When he comes to you with a word he cannot say, don't just say it for him; rather, help him sound it out.

- There are numerous fun and challenging books and games sold in book stores and on the Internet that will help the child along.

Main Idea

- Being able to know the main idea of the story will improve as the child's comprehension develops. Usually, the title will give the main idea of the story.

- Look at the picture on the cover of the book and read the title to your child before you begin to read. That is what the book will be all about. For example, in the book, "Bears Like to Dance," the main idea would be about bears.

- As you read, every now and then stop and ask the child to tell you about what you have already read, and what he thinks will happen next, or predict how the story will end. This will sharpen his focus on the story. Help him along if he stumbles in his replies.

Vocabulary

An extensive vocabulary is needed for comprehension. What good is it for a student to decode words because he knows the sounds of the letters, but does not understand the meaning of the words? Do you remember times when you attempted to read an article or book that was "over your head" because you didn't understand many of the vocabulary words?

- *You don't need to teach your child vocabulary words. Your child will repeat what he hears from you. If you use plain, simple, over-used words like big, little, or pretty, he will use those words. If you use more sophisticated words like attractive, enormous, and trivial, he will use them also.* Following are a number of word pairs. Try making a list of several pairs and tack them to your kitchen wall. Challenge yourself to use the words when talking to your child or other family members. Create conversations in which you would use them. A good example could be when your child is late coming home from school, you would ask him for his alibi, instead of excuse. In time, your child will have an extensive vocabulary. Simple!

excuse	alibi	alone	isolated
start	embark	ask	enquire
dry	arid	beg	plead
alone	isolated	dig	excavate
family	clan	hot	torrid
shout	bellow	busy	occupied

fang	tusk	mud	mire
odor	essence	ring	peal
fat	stout	thirsty	parched
stink	reek	zoo	menagerie
look	gaze	noise	uproar
storm	tempest	sharp	keen
warm	tepid	smell	whiff
trick	prank	thin	scrawny
speedy	rapid	corner	niche
home	abode	large	vast

Sequence of Events

Mastering the sequence skills is crucial to reading comprehension. It helps us break down past events into logical order of how they happened. It is also needed to give directions and to remember the steps to perform certain tasks that need to be done in a specific order. We need sequencing skills to help us organize ideas and information, to help us solve problems, and to understand scientific information. The ability to understand sequence takes a long time and will develop as the child matures and becomes a more proficient reader. Meanwhile, here are suggestions to help its development while reading and talking to him.

- Have him tell you about his experiences in the order in which they happened, such as at a birthday party: did they play games first, when did the child open his presents, when did they have refreshments. Whenever your child goes somewhere, ask him to tell you about what he did, in order. If he goes to a movie, ask him to tell you about it. Ask him to tell you about what he did in school.

- Read an old story book to him, then tear the pages out, mix them up and let the child put them in the order in which they took place. Do the same with the newspaper cartoons. Then let the child show you the pictures one at a time, and tell you about the story or cartoon in his own words. Help him if needed.

- While reading, keep going back to events that happened before. Have him recall parts of the story already read. Ask him what happened first, then next, and then after that, up to where you are presently reading. This keeps him thinking, helps clarify situations and parts characters play in relation to others.

- While reading, emphasize words that indicate time of events, such as then, first,

- last, now, finally, and next.

- Use these words when telling him to perform certain tasks in the order of which they must be done, such as getting ready for bed: first take off your dirty clothes and put them in the hamper, next wash up and brush your teeth, then put on your pajamas, and finally pick out a book for your bedtime story.

- Purchase some of the delightful, reasonably priced sequencing games and activities found in book stores and online.

Drawing Conclusions

Asking the child what he thinks will happen next in a story will not only encourage comprehension, but he'll have to give it some serious thought, and weigh his answer on what he has already read. If his comprehension is not good, he won't be able to answer the question. Have patience… remember, he doesn't already have these skills, he's learning them.

- While reading, pause often to ask the child what he thinks will happen next. To keep the question from becoming monotonous, make a game of it. Both of you take a guess. Fake it so you will be wrong some of the time. Praise your child when he's right. Make comments such as, "You're right again!" "You're getting pretty good at this!" "Hey, you're really paying attention!"

- "Why" questions have a strong influence on comprehension. Questions such as, "Why is it thundering?" "Why is the dog barking?" "Why did the bird fly away?" "Why is your hair mussed up?" and, "Why is the monkey chattering?" are all thought-provoking questions based on what happened previously. The child will love to answer these questions and will consider it a game. At first he'll probably hem and haw, not knowing what to say. But with encouragement and practice, he'll soon be giving answers every time, some accurate, some just guesswork. Accept any sensible answer. Have fun!

- "Because" statements stimulate the brain in a similar fashion. The child has to make inferences in order to answer logically. His answer must be the result of reasoning. Instead of beginning with why, make a partial statement, and wait for the child to complete it with the right answer. For example, "We could not go for our walk today, because…it started to rain." "The puppy soiled the carpet, because… we forgot to take him outside." "The soup tasted bland, because…

- mother forgot to put in the salt." "The ice cream melted, because... it wasn't put back in the freezer." Initially, you would ask the why part and your child would supply the answer. When the child catches on, you can switch roles and let him ask the why questions. Very challenging. Keep it fun!

- While reading together, help the child identify emotions. Anger, sadness, jealousy, happiness, hurt, disappointment, and frustration are all emotions the child either has already experienced or soon will. Being able to identify them in characters he is reading about will help him understand the feelings when he experiences them himself. Ask him what caused these particular feelings, and what the character could have done to prevent them if they were negative. Discuss how healthy people control their negative emotions, and what the child could do when he feels that way. The child who comprehends is able to relate to the feelings of the characters or animals with regard to the situations that caused the feelings. At the same time, you can help the child empathize with people in real life situations, such as a crying baby, an elderly person who is cranky, handicapped people, street people, children who are made fun of by their peers, and animals that are mistreated. Many adults never do acquire this skill, which is very dependent upon comprehension.

Chapter 18

FOLLOWING DIRECTIONS

"Listen, Pay Attention, Concentrate!
If everything else fails, read the instructions."

Ralph Waldo Emerson

Poor Comprehension

Children with poor comprehension skills have difficulty following directions because they don't understand what was said or they don't listen properly. Some of my fourth grade students could not read and follow simple instructions, such as, "Write your name in the top right corner of the paper.**" A lack of listening and attention skills is a major roadblock to children's reading comprehension.** It becomes a real problem when they're in school and supposed to follow their teachers' directions or independently read and follow the directions for an assignment. *A child must be able to listen, understand what was said, and then act on what he heard. These are critical skills for school success.*

Teaching a child to follow directions seems so trivial… you would think that it should just come naturally to him, especially when you ask him to do something several times a day. But think back about the many times he's not paying attention, and you have to repeat yourself, or he doesn't hear everything you say and is not able to obey you. Children's attention span will improve with age, and eventually they become good listeners when they're motivated. However, *the more practice young children receive at home at listening and following directions, the better students they will become. Parents should not leave development of these skills up to chance. When you think about it, there are dozens of daily opportunities for you to give your child practice, whether it's with personal responsibilities, chores around the house, or just a matter of doing things for you when needed.*

However, *there are right ways and wrong ways to give your child instructions to do anything, and most of us give instructions the wrong way. Until you learn how to give your child instructions properly, you must refrain from complaining that he doesn't listen to you.* I remember so often scolding my kids for not listening to me, and punishing them for not obeying me, when all along, they just did not connect with what I told them to do.

Poor Attention Skills

Before you can expect your child to obey you, you must first make certain he hears you. Surely you've heard the expression, "It went in one ear and out the other." Chances are, he didn't hear your instructions in the first place, or he wasn't paying attention when you told him to do something. Here are several ways to improve your requests to your child:

1. ***Most important is to eliminate any distractions,*** such as television, playing with toys, games, or reading a book. It would be best to *call him to you*, away from what he is doing, or temporarily take away whatever it is that has his attention.

2. ***Make him look at you*** so he isn't looking at something else that will prevent him from concentrating on what you're saying. If it appears that you don't have his attention, you may have to take him by the shoulders or put your hands on his face and turn it towards yours and say, *"I want you to listen to what I have to tell you."* Give him several seconds to focus on what you are going to say before you give him instructions. ***Tell him what you want him to do and then ask him to repeat what you said.***

3. Be careful not to group several things together that you want him to do. Rather than tell him to clean up his room, ***it's better to take him there and point out the things he needs to do*** to make his room tidy, such as hang up his clothes, put his shoes in the closet, put his toys away, and put his books on the shelf.

4. It's better to ask a younger child to do just one or two things at a time until he's older and demonstrates that he is capable of doing more. You might ask an older child to do up to three or four things at a time and number them. For example, when calling him in from playing outdoors, stop him by the door when he's coming in and say: "There are three things I want you to do: one, hang up your jacket, two, wash your hands, and three, set the table. Do you think you can do all those things?" Most likely, he will, ***especially if you make him focus on what you were going to say.***

5. Always follow up with a hug or positive comment when your child listens and does what he is told. If he forgets or doesn't do what you ask, remind him that he didn't pay attention when you asked him to do something. Perhaps a scolding may be in order. Teaching your child to listen is just like any other behavior you want him to learn.

6. Praise will go a long way toward cooperation and the child's desire to please you, but if you made your request clear, and he deliberately disobeyed you, then consequences would be in order.

Miscellaneous Directions

Explain to your older child why following directions is so important in school and life. For him to learn to read or do math, play the guitar or basketball, use a cell phone, drive a car, or build a house, he must be able to pay attention and follow directions. Tell him you will be asking him many times throughout the day to do things, find things, and bring things to you that will help him build these skills, and you want him to try really hard to cooperate.

Suggest you make a game out of the child paying attention. Give the game a name, or say a key word, such as "listen," loudly when you want the child to do something. Whenever the child hears the word, he is to stop what he is doing and pay attention or come to where you are. Then challenge him to listen to you closely, repeat what you told him to do, then follow through with your request. Be sure to praise him for listening to you and following your directions. Remind him every morning when he goes to school to look at his teacher and listen to what she has to say. Here are some examples of the numerous directions parents probably already give throughout their day. If the kids don't follow through or forget halfway before doing everything, perhaps you didn't give the directions properly.

- Give simple one-step directions to the toddler, such as to put the ball in the toy box, his shoes in the closet, or the book on the shelf." You may be able to give the preschool child two things to do.

- Give the older child more complicated two-part directions, such as, "Place your socks in the top drawer of your dresser, and your T-shirts in the middle drawer."

- Hang your blouses on the left side of the closet, your jeans on the right side, and put your sweaters in the drawer.

- Move the chairs away from the table, sweep the floor, then put the chairs back.

- Take out the trash, hang up your jacket and put your books on the shelf.

- Go the bathroom and look in the second drawer and bring me a Q-tip. I also need the tweezers that are in a box in the top drawer.

- Go out in the car and get the flashlight from the glove box. Bring it in and replace its batteries. Be sure you put it back in the glove box, so we'll have it when we need it.

- While putting groceries away, ask her to put the toothpaste in the second drawer in the bathroom, the soap in the third drawer, and the tissues on bottom drawer of the hall closet.

- Go out in the garage and look in the nail drawers and see if you can find me a 2" long flat headed nail; bring me the hammer, too.

- Be sure you tell him to "listen" before you tell him what to do, or his mind might be on something else and he won't hear you.

- Keep these activities fun by joking when he forgets and praising him when he succeeds. You might say things like, "You're not listening!" or, "Good job!"

More challenging forms of directions for the older child can be in three or four parts. In my home, we had storage shelves in the basement where I placed excess food and other items I didn't have room for upstairs. Asking any one of my kids to go downstairs and look for a can of tomato juice on the left side of the bottom shelf, next to the canned vegetables, or some similar item, usually ended up in repeated directions and numerous "I can't find its." Out of frustration I usually had to go down to get it myself. Most kids would forget what you tell them before they get halfway down the stairs. Kids will find directions such as these to be mind-boggling. It would help if you numbered them and had the child repeat them before he attempts to follow them.

Following are a number of games your kids will love to play while reinforcing their direction following skills:

Games to Reinforce Following Directions Skills:

- **Hiding Coins** – Give step-by-step directions on how to find them. "There's a nickel (for the preschooler) in your bedroom beneath the red book on the book shelf." Let him keep it if he finds it, even if he needs additional directions. Make the directions more difficult for the older child and the reward larger.

- **Treasure Hunt** – Accumulate small toys and other objects your child would enjoy, such as stickers, new pencils, gum, note tablets, a new box of crayons, and pencil top erasers, any of which may be used as the treasure. Nickels, dimes, and quarters would also be highly motivating. Place an item in a small treasure box and hide it. Give him the first note, which tells him where to go for the 2nd note. Plant notes in several places. Each note tells him where to go next and finally leads him to the treasure. Examples: Note one: "Look under the

- first cushion on the sofa." Note two: "Go to your bedroom and look inside of the white tennis shoes." Note three: "Look under the dog's water dish." Note four: "Go to the bookshelves and look under the dictionary." Note five is in the (empty) slow cooker (which is where the treasure could be).

- **Direction Drawing** – Give her crayons and a blank piece of paper. Caution her to listen carefully. Give her the following instructions. Pin her completed paper on the wall.

  1. Draw a circle in the middle of your paper.
     Draw a green line down the center of the circle.
     Color the right side of the circle red.
     Put 2 little circles in the left side.
     Color one circle purple and the other circle orange.

  2. Fold another paper in half, and then fold it in half again.
     Number the squares from left to right, top to bottom.
     Color number 3 red.
     Put a black X in number 1.
     Draw a smiling face in number 2.
     Put 5 purple dots in number 4.

  3. Fold a blank paper in half, and then fold it in half again.
     Draw a doll wearing a red hat in square 1.
     Draw a yellow daisy in square 4.
     Draw a green and orange striped lollipop in square 3.
     Draw a smiley face in square 2.

- **Coloring** – This can be done with one child or more than one. Copy a page for each child from a coloring book. You can do this with the child or pre-color the picture ahead of time. Give oral instructions to color the objects, such as the flower black, the house green, the windows purple, and so on. Make the objects unconventional colors so he can't guess the right color.

- **Following a Recipe** – Cooking and following a recipe is an excellent way to practice following directions. Read the recipe together with the school-aged child before you begin. Then let him say what to do first, second, third, and so on. When he's old enough, let him bake and cook himself with your guidance.

- **Cereal Boxes** – Many cereal boxes have little gadgets and games enclosed which come with directions on how to assemble them or how to play the game. Let your child read and follow the directions himself or read them together while you help him.

- **Assemblage Directions** – Just about everything you purchase comes with a set of directions: many toys and games, television sets, cell phones, microwaves, cleaning supplies, cooking supplies, wallpaper, cameras, paint, tools of all kinds, and so on. Get your child involved with you whenever you have to read directions. If he's a beginning reader, have him with you while you read the directions, and then do the assembling together. If you buy him a bicycle, you will have to put it together for him, but he should be involved in helping you. Have him read and follow a portion of the directions while you follow them together.

I remember how I froze when my son and I purchased a treadmill and saw the booklet of instructions to assemble it. Neither of us was experienced in putting machines together, but it was either pay a handyman to do it or assemble it ourselves. So we went to work, and through trial and error, we put it together! It was a great lesson for us, because we realized that all we had to do was study the instructions and illustrations, sometimes read them two or three times, and we could put together what we wanted.

Memory

In order to be successful learners, children must be able to concentrate (pay attention), comprehend (understand) and retain information, in order to be able to recall it when needed. These brain skills are needed in all areas of life. The more practice the child gets using his memory at home, the easier it will be for him to handle the information waiting for him to learn in school and adult life. Rather than wait until the child's memory strengthens with age, parents can give him a great head start through simple, easy to do activities and they'll have fun with them while they're at it.

Daily Memory Building

From the toddler age to well into grade school, parents can help the child build his memory by asking questions that will require him to remember details of events he experienced himself or from stories his parents read to him. *This practice can be built into their daily parent/child contact.*

Here are some examples:

- Recall characters and events from a story you read to the child.

- Point out objects and people on a book page. Then turn the page and see how many she can remember. Praise her and write them down.

- When you run errands, challenge her to recall, in chronological order, all of the places you went, such as the cleaners, mechanic, bank, grocery store, or credit union.

- Before your child goes to a party, tell him you want to hear all about what it was like, such as what games they played, what refreshments were served, what flavor the cake was, what were some of the presents, and who else was there.

- Ask him what games he played at recess and with whom, who he ate lunch with, or what math concept he learned that day.

Games and Fun Activities That Build Memory Skills

- Ask your child to study you and your appearance. (This is great fun!) Then have her turn away or blindfold her and ask her questions, such as: "What is the color of the shirt I am wearing?" "Does my shirt have long or short sleeves?" "What jewelry am I wearing?" "Do I have polish on my nails?" "Am I wearing lipstick?" "What kind of shoes am I wearing?" "Was I holding anything in my hands?" At first, have her concentrate on just what she sees above your waist or just on your head.

- Fill a little bag with several small objects such as a thread spool, crayon, paper clip, pencil, eraser, screw, plant hook, clothespin, plastic twisty, and button. Set three or four objects on the table and let the child look at them for sixty seconds. Then have her close her eyes while you remove one item. See if she can remember which one is missing.

- Set three or four items on the table and let the child study their positions. Have her close her eyes while you rearrange the items. Then have her open her eyes and put the items back into their original formation. Use more objects for the older child.

- Use the same bag of objects. Let the blindfolded child reach inside and remove an object. He is to tell you what it is by the way it feels while he's still blindfolded.

- Send the child to a room to study the furnishings for ten minutes. Offer him a nickel for each item he can recall, orally or in a drawing. Everything within the room counts: patterns in wallpaper, cracks in walls, dressers, drawers, knobs, tile, fixtures, and so on. It may be easier to draw a picture or make a list. When he's finished, let him describe the picture in detail to you. Go with him to the first room and help him so he understands what to do.

- Send the child outside to observe the characteristics of the house and yard. Go with her, focusing her attention on the windows, doors, porch, railings, trim, stucco, frame, and all visible details. Return to the inside drawing table and have her draw and color a picture of the house and yard with as much detail as she can remember.

- Give your child a section of the newspaper and show her how to skim for a certain word. Then challenge her to circle all instances of the words and or the in one minute. She'll have to keep her mind set on this one activity and nothing else. Other words could be contractions, pronouns, or names.

- Playing card games like Fish, Steal the Bundle, Crazy Eights and Pig will strengthen memory, concentration and attention skills. These are great after dinner activities (after homework) instead of watching television.

Chapter 19

READING INCENTIVES

"Reading should not be presented to children as a chore or duty.

It should be offered to them as a precious gift."

Kate DiCamillo, American Writer

Learning to read is very tedious. *It takes students years of struggling to learn the alphabet, decode words, and comprehend well enough to be an independent reader. Although they may be learning to read as well as expected, you still have to give them one-on-one assistance, and keep nagging them to read, read, read. They resist reading because it's difficult, and it's no fun. But they won't get better unless they read a lot.* Rather than continuous nagging, you can help your child reach the enjoyable and independent reading stage by enticing her to read more with fun and rewarding activities.

Below are a number of incentives you can use. When she becomes bored with one activity,   substitute another one that will keep her motivated. Whatever activity you select, be sure you set some rules about the size of the books she must read, so she's not tempted to read short, unchallenging ones. It's very important for an adult to be available to help the child with words she can't pronounce or doesn't understand.   If she's reading independently, be sure to verify she's actually reading the books rather than just breezing through in order to claim another book read. To make certain she's benefiting, have her tell you about each book she reads. Kids can be very tricky. If she's cheating, then take away the incentives for a while.

Book Chains – Cut a number of 1 ½" x 5" strips of white construction paper. Each book the child reads will be a link of the book chain. Have her write the title of the book on the strip, decorate or color the strip any way she chooses, then staple the ends together to form a circle. Each subsequent link should be attached to the one before it in order to form the chain. Begin the chain anywhere she wants, dangling from her bedroom ceiling or on the kitchen wall. If there's more than one child, let them work together, even get the entire family involved. Give each member a different color so everyone can see at a glance how many books each has read. Children who are reading larger or more difficult books that take longer to complete may get to add a link for reading 10 or 20 pages. Parents may participate, also with their own chains, or add their color to the child's chain. Decide what counts besides books, such as newspapers and magazines.

Reading Quilt – The more people involved in this activity the more fun it is. For each book completed, the person gets to add a patch to the quilt, which would be an 8 ½" x 11" piece of white paper, or if you have a way to cut it into an even square, that would be better. Color and decorate it in some way that is related to the story or characters, such as a dog, sailboat, etc. On the back write the title. Have the family members sit together, and listen to the child tell about the story before she attaches her section to the quilt, which can be on a wall, perhaps in the hallway, or even the front room. A good time to tell about a story is when the family is together having dinner.

Stickers – These are great to use as motivators and also rewards for any type of good work or behavior. Give your child a sticker for each book he reads. When he completes the book, let him draw a picture related to the story and tell you about it. Put the sticker on the picture and pin it on a wall. Stickers may be purchased at book stores, dollar stores, or Walmart. I could get my 4th grade students to do anything for a sticker. Imagine 25 students tip-toeing down the school hall (so they wouldn't bother students in other classrooms) to the restroom and back without talking, just to get a sticker for being quiet when they got back.

Hole Puncher – For the beginning reader, give him a strip of construction paper to use as a bookmark and let him punch a hole in it for each fifteen minutes he reads or each book he reads. Chances are, he won't want to quit after fifteen minutes; however, insist that in order to punch a hole, he must read in a fifteen-minute block. If he passes fifteen minutes, and reads another five, it doesn't count for another time. Encourage him to read just ten more minutes, and he will get to punch two holes in the bookmark. After reading four hours in bits and pieces he should receive a reward of some kind, perhaps a sticker, a new pencil, or eraser.

Calendars – Calendars are versatile motivators. Give the child a star or smiley face to put in the day's square, or let him color in the box for each block of fifteen minutes he reads. Give him a treat or small reward when he fills in a week or more, a larger reward for the month.   For the older child who is capable of reading more, the requirement should be perhaps a half hour or an entire book.

Apple Tree – With colored chalk, draw a picture of a tree with branches on the wall. Let your child cut out a number of apples from red construction paper, or she can make her own and decorate it.   Let her tape an apple on the tree for each book she reads. This, too, can be a family project and may include reading the newspapers or a magazine.

Bookworms – Draw the head of a bookworm and make a number of segments for its body. The child would write the title of her completed book on a segment and attach it to the worm. Small children really enjoy this when they can stretch the worm's body across the wall.

Fish Tank – Draw a large fish tank on the wall about 3' x 6'. Let the child draw and color a fish to add to the tank for each book she reads. This can lead to a nice art project for the child. Look up tropical fish on the Internet or check out a library book about fish. The child will read even more to learn about the aquatic life of fish before she completes her project. Fill in the name of the book on the back of the fish.

Footprints – Let the child make a footprint for each book she reads by tracing her tennis shoe on a piece of white construction paper. Then copy the design on the bottom of the shoe onto her paper copy. Print the title on the other side. Color the pattern and then cut it out. Place markers representing a starting point somewhere on the wall, and another for a finish line somewhere on the ceiling, perhaps in another room. Let the child place her footprints heading toward the finish line. Determine how far apart they may be. I did this with my classroom, and we had footprints on the ceiling going out the room and down the hall to the office. What fun!

Read-a-Thon – Suggest charitable reading to earn money to donate to unfortunate people, or to raise money for a good cause. Help your child decide. Make her aware of articles in the paper about unfortunate families or beneficial programs, such as Friends of the Library, Muscular Dystrophy Foundation, or animal shelters. She would ask family and friends to sponsor her and pay so much towards the charity for each book she reads. Consider allowing her to get two or three friends involved, as well.

Tickets – This is a great motivator. Give your child a clear, plastic jar, such as one from peanut butter or salad dressing. Give your child a ticket each time he reads a book. You can purchase tickets from the dollar store or make them yourself. When he gets several, give a promised reward.

Money Bank – Giving money is one of the greatest motivators, especially if your child is old enough to understand its value. A dollar for a book that takes several sessions to finish sounds about right and twenty five cents for 15 minutes sessions. Be sure you take the child to the dollar store to select a small toy when he has enough money to spend.

You might feel your way when it comes to rewards. I would be inclined to first try having a special pizza party with friends after he reads perhaps twenty books, or ten if that's too many. But make him work for it. If that isn't incentive enough, then consider a material reward that he would like to have.

Utilizing just a few of these motivators will keep your child reading until you don't have to motivate her any more. You can even use them for other behaviors, such as

family chores, papers with good marks, keeping the bedroom clean, not fighting or arguing with siblings, or whatever habit you want him to break or establish. Just the fun and challenge he'll get from reading with these incentives will replace any material rewards. And before you know it, you won't have to nag him to read anymore. He'll read because he enjoys the stories.

Chapter 20

HOME WRITING ACTIVITIES

"Ideal communication must be an exchange of thought, and not, as many of those who worry most about their shortcomings believe, an eloquent exhibition of wit or oratory."

Emily Post

The Cursive Controversy

There's much debate today about whether or not to teach students cursive in schools. Teachers maintain that by excluding cursive they will have time to teach more important subjects. And besides, since most communication today is done through technology, ***teaching students to communicate through said technology is most critical.***

Child development experts maintain that cursive writing helps small children develop hand-eye coordination, fine motor skills, and other brain and memory functions, such as reasoning, problem solving and conceptualization. Virginia Berninger, a professor of educational psychology at the University of Washington, has shown that printing, cursive, and keyboarding activate different brain patterns, and that ***in some cases, students with certain disabilities may struggle with print, but do well with cursive. According to a 2014 New York Times article, researchers are finding that teaching children cursive may help treat dyslexia.***

And so the debate goes on. Teachers have tremendous responsibilities and could apply their extra time to teaching communication through technology; however, a great part of communication by many people, colleges, businesses, and employers is through cursive writing. Once adulthood is reached, lack of ability to read and write cursive could be a great loss.

Look at it this way: if the school your child attends teaches cursive, then support it. If the school doesn't, that's o.k., too. The younger generation today hardly ever uses cursive, so your children won't miss it. Considering cognitive development, just make certain your child has ample opportunities to be involved in eye-hand coordination activities. If you really want your child to know cursive and his school doesn't teach it, then teach him at home. There are a number of booklets on the market that will give your child practice with cursive writing. My suggestions are for either printing or cursive writing. You can start with printing and cursive in the early years and when the child is ready, transition him to the computer.

Preschool – Print Awareness

Writing is putting one's thoughts and feelings into words and then putting them on paper. Before children can read and write, they must first develop an understanding of the connection of thoughts, words, and print. This must happen during their preschool years because it forms the basis for literacy instruction, which begins when they enter school. Until then, drawing and scribbling are their way of communicating. The scrib bling stage is usually from ages two to three, then during their fourth and fifth years their art begins to take on recognizable people and objects. It's during these later years that they begin to associate the words they've been hearing with the words they have been seeing in print.

It's never too early to begin teaching children how to write, and parents can give them a good head start at home. Begin as soon as the child shows an interest in scribbling. Her artwork will be messy, so make sure you have a place where she can use a wide range of supplies without fear of getting things dirty or out of place. I would suggest a closet-size door propped up with cinder blocks which would be low enough for her to sit at comfortably. You can make it washable by painting it. Find some shelves from Walmart or the thrift store on which to place paper, large crayons, markers, paint, brushes, and finger paints. Newspaper is excellent for markers or water colors. Spend time drawing with your child, showing her how to use the different supplies, beginning with just one, such as crayons or marking pens. At another time introduce the finger paints, and then the water colors when she's old enough. You can teach her to clean up her mess and keep the shelves organized at the same time.

Following are a number of strategies parents can use to help prepare their children for reading and writing literacy when they enter school:

- *Words Abound* – The more printed words the child sees, the closer she will be to *print awareness* – that is understanding that the words we speak are represented by printed words. Make your home "print-rich" by making signs to attach to objects in your kitchen, where you and your child are most often together. Seeing words, such as *wall, table, cabinet, window, refrigerator, or chair* will help her understand that they have verbal connections and will fit right into learning words by sight. Just in your home alone, there are endless objects with labels that show print, such as toothpaste, coffee, milk, etc. Point these words out to her whenever possible.

- *Alphabet Association* –When you begin to teach your child the alphabet, have colorful pictures taped to the kitchen wall showing objects beginning with the letter your child is learning. For example, if learning the letter and sound of B, show pictures of B words, such as banana, baby or ball. Look for the letters she's learning in the text of the book you read to her. Refer to these pictures and the words often. Find them on cereal boxes, in magazines, and newspapers.

- ***While Reading*** – Begin every story by looking at the cover and reading the title while pointing to the words. Show the child the author's and illustrator's names. While reading, move your finger under the words from left to right, and back to the left again. Show him when you reach the bottom and where you begin at the top of the next page. Every now and then, point to words that name pictures of people, animals, and objects. For example, while reading about a horse, point to the word and sound it out, saying "This word spells horse." And when you come across a familiar word like "Mommy," point to the letters while sounding them out.

- ***Modeling*** – Throughout your days, you probably jot down notes numerous times: your grocery list, errands to make, places you need to go, appointments on calendars, writing checks to pay bills, addressing envelopes, and so on. Let your child observe you writing whenever possible. She'll begin to copy you while she's playing and it will help her associate the written word with what she hears.

- ***Tracing Letters*** – The finger coordination of preschool children is just beginning to develop, so don't expect legible writing; however, as a deviation from scribbles and drawing, show your child how to trace over the printed letters of the alphabet she's learning, and how to print her name. Print the letters at least 6" high and let her use her choice of crayons. There are also numerous commercial alphabet books that provide this practice. This will help her coordination along, but don't let this take the place of her creative drawings.

- ***Dictation and Writing*** – Any adult or older sibling can act as the child's assistant as soon as she is able to tell you about her drawings. When she draws a scribble, ask her to tell you what it is, write her exact words, repeating each one, and then read them aloud while pointing to them. You'll be amazed at some of the stories you will hear. I remember the black, yellow, and blue colored scribble my three-year-old daughter brought to me. When asked what it was, she told me it was a group of bees that took off their clothes to go swimming. A caption under this picture could be, "The bees are swimming." Or she might say, "The bees took off their clothes so they wouldn't get wet." This is the first stage of the child's reading and writing process. This form of dictation will greatly help the child toward print awareness.

- ***Homemade Books*** – Provide your child with a book in which to draw her pic

- tures. She can call it, "My Story Book." She can draw pictures on the pages and then dictate what she wants you to write as a caption underneath, just like the newspaper or comic book cartoons.

Here are three simple and inexpensive home-made books:

1. Fold clean computer pages in half and staple them up the middle. Then fold them back and you have a little book. Let the child write, "My Picture Book," on the cover. Inside, write her name as the author and illustrator.

2. Purchase plastic covers with colored ribs that slide up the edges of several pages together. School children use these to encase their reports or essays. They are inexpensive and have the desirable aspect of allowing the cover with its name and drawing to show through the plastic. They're ideal for children's drawings and stories.

3. Purchase a spiral notebook with blank pages on which to draw her pictures.

Preschool and School Ages

- *Captioned Drawings* – Encourage the child to compose a sentence or small paragraph to accompany her drawings. Let the preschool child dictate to you what she wants to say. It can be written in comic book fashion or in block form underneath the picture. The child may also enjoy writing about cut pictures from magazines. Let him paste them in a booklet with a caption about the picture. For example, if it's a picture of a Disneyland character, the child's sentence could be, "Barney is dancing," or "Muriel is singing." If it's a dog eating, it could be, "The dog is eating his dinner." You would have to print this for the younger child.

- *All Occasion Cards* – Suggest your children make gifts for their loved ones. I loved the cards and little gifts my children made for me. Supply them with the materials and let them use their creativity to produce cards and gifts that will be forever cherished. Help them write poems or messages within the cards.

- *Thank-You Notes, Cards, and Letters* – The acceptance of a gift should always require an acknowledgement, no matter how young the child. Make the suggestion, then supply the materials. The school-age child can draw a picture, and compose a note about what she liked about the gift. The preschooler can draw a picture and tell you what she liked about the gift while you write what she says.

- *Santa Claus Letter* – You won't have to motivate your child to write a letter to Santa Claus…he'll pester you until you help him. The preschooler can dictate what he wants while you print his words for him. He can also draw or scribble pictures of what he would like. The older child should write the letter in proper form.

School-Age – Grades Three to Six

Obstacles to Writing

Students usually are introduced to writing simple sentences in first grade. At that time, they are taught to capitalize the first word, spell correctly and to put a period at the end. Gradually, as they advance, they are taught to use commas with compound sentences, question and exclamation marks. But all this is taught on a small scale, so they are able to concentrate on the correct way to write short sentences. However, **when they get into the middle grades and begin to write paragraphs, essays, and stories, it can be overwhelming for them to have to think, write, spell correctly, put in capitals, and end their sentences with a period, exclamation mark, or question mark.** When this happens, they lose concentration on what they want to write, which causes them to lose motivation. This is what prevents many students from developing advanced writing skills.

Simple Writing Procedure

Teaching children how to write can be very simple. First they need to be motivated to think about something fun and exciting to write. Then write their story in their own words as they think about it until they reach the end. *During this writing time, they are not to be stressed about spelling, or worry about what kind of punctuation to use. The biggest hurdle for them to get over is to begin feeling comfortable about putting their thoughts and ideas into words and writing them down on paper, just as though they are telling someone their story.*

When finished writing, they would then go back and concentrate on making their sentences as correct as they are able. The first copy is considered a *rough draft* on which they will make corrections. At this stage, they look for words they know how to spell correctly, begin the sentences with capital letters, and make certain their sentences make sense. A parent or older sibling should be available to help proofread for correct spelling and legible sentences. But don't strive for perfection. It takes time to make writing grammatically correct, spell properly, and put punctuation where it belongs.

These skills will come gradually with age and more effort. Following is the procedure I recommend to you to encourage your child to write at home. It may seem like a lot to you, but it needn't be. Work on one sentence at first, build up to a paragraph, and then a story.

- Accept what the child produces. A beginning writer or an older one who is having difficulty may write only a few sentences or a paragraph. Through your prodding and suggestions, the more he writes, the better he will get. Don't criticize his work as being too short, not enough, or having too many mistakes.

- Praise the story and express sincere interest. Ask questions that may contribute to improvement when the child writes his good copy, such as "What color was the wagon?" "Who lived in the house?" "What was the dog's name?"

- If he writes a simple sentence such as, "The dog barked," ask if the dog was angry or excited, and at whom it was barking. Help him to make his sentences more interesting such as, "The angry dog barked at the frightened man." Then select a word to look up in the Thesaurus to change to a more sophisticated one, such as, "The angry cur barked."

- When finished with his rough draft, help him look for mistakes in spelling, punctuation, and sensible sentences. Help him find his own mistakes, but do not proofread for him. Have him read each sentence to you. Does it make sense? Does it sound as if he is speaking? If not, what word is missing. How can he make it better? Is it missing a capital letter or period? Are any words misspelled? Soon he will be able to proofread himself, and the time will come, *perhaps not until high school, that he will be able to write and proofread an almost perfect copy.*

- Remember, keep it short for the beginner. If he writes a real neat long story, cherish it just the way he wrote it. Have him punctuate only what his ability allows. *Don't let proofreading get stressful.*

- Ask the child to draw a picture to go with his story, and then read it to the family. Tape it to the wall.

- Praise both his finished and proofread copies. He worked hard on them. Keep his stories in a notebook to compare improvement at the end of the school year.

Journals

Children need to be taught about their emotions, rather than just experiencing them in bewilderment. Writing about them would not only help them understand their feelings, but would also give them excellent writing practice. Give your child a notebook with dividers. Have sections for anger, happiness, pride, hurt feelings, sadness, or embarrassment. Dreams and friendships may be popular topics as well. Encourage her to write for perhaps fifteen minutes a day in whatever area she chooses, which may turn into thirty or more when she's motivated. You'll have to help her at first. You may even have to encourage her with incentives, such as stars on a calendar, or a quarter for each entry she makes.

- To get her started, watch for examples of various emotions as they happen and explain them to her. Then help her write about her experience that caused her to feel that way.

- Describing your own feelings will help your child understand hers when she first experiences them. Telling my students about my embarrassing experience when a large group of people witnessed me accidentally walk into a men's restroom gave them a good laugh, and made them feel more relaxed about their own embarrassing moments.

- You may witness two car drivers honking and shouting at each other, or a driver rudely honking the horn at someone he thought was driving too slow.

- Your child may have been proud or elated if she won a contest, gave a nice presentation in Science class, or was selected for the volleyball team.

- She may have been embarrassed when she tripped and fell in front of the class, or felt humiliated when her teacher scolded her for talking in class.

- Perhaps he was sad and hurt, because he was ridiculed on the playground, or proud when he swam in the deep end of the swimming pool for the first time. Encourage him to discuss his feelings.

- While viewing a movie or television program, watch for various emotions being displayed by the characters, even animals. Discuss them with your child and the reasons that brought them about.

- Another great way to identify emotions would be to ask the child how charac

- ters may feel in the story you are reading together.

Writing Lists

There's always a time when the kids don't have anything to do, especially on weekends or summer vacation when they shouldn't watch too much television. Suggest they write a list. You might make it more challenging by offering a nickel for each item they include. If there're more than one child close to the same age, let them compete to see who can write the most items. The topics are endless.

furniture in the house	kitchen items
clothes in the closet	games to play
fruits and vegetables	desserts
toys in her room	animals
books on the shelf	home items in alphabetical order
names of classmates	objects beginning with the same letter

Picture Writing

Uninhibited children write the most delightful stories, but you can't just suggest that they write a story…you need to motivate them…give them something to visualize and think about. One of my students' favorite stories to write about was creatures from outer space. They would draw and color a creature. Then write a story while answering questions I suggested, such as where it came from, how it came to earth, did it have a family, what type of food would it find to eat here on earth, could it be lost, did it ever find its family and go back to its planet, or did it find a home here on earth. By this time the children were all busy writing with excitement.

When they finish their rough drafts, help them proofread. You never have to motivate a child to draw a picture to go with his story. He may want to draw and color it first, while he's thinking of a story to write. Let him practice reading his story with expression into the tape recorder. Then play it for the family. Display the story and picture on the wall.

Make a file of motivating pictures to use to get your child to write stories. This is a great rainy day activity, or one when the child is driving you crazy and you're so tempted to turn on the television. Look for motivating pictures in newspapers or magazines you receive.

Story Starters

Other ways to motivate the child is to give him a *start* to a story or a topic. Following are a number of delightful *Story Starters* you can use. Be certain to help him get started by asking several questions to give him something to think about.

- How Did the Zebra Get its Stripes?
- How Did the Elephant Get its Trunk?
- How Did the Pig's Tail Get its Curl?
- The First Fish I Caught
- My Nightmare
- When I Foiled a Bank Robbery
- A Job I Hate to Do and Why
- The Living Snowman
- The Cave
- My Most Embarrassing Moment
- Bugs Everywhere!
- A Huge Creature Suddenly Jumped out at Me!
- There Once Was a Bear…
- My Visit to McDonalds
- The Ghost Family
- How to Bathe your Dog (in sequence)
- I Wish…
- How to Make your Favorite Sandwich
- If I Had Three Wishes
- A happy Moment in My Life
- What Does the Tooth Fairy Do with the Teeth she finds under the pillows?
- My Friend, the Giant

Chapter 21

EDUCATIONAL FUN

"Imagination is More Important than Knowledge."

Albert Einstein

What do you do with your kids when they have nothing to do and they can't watch television? They'll drive you crazy, either fighting with each other or nagging for something to do, hoping you'll let them turn on the TV. How tempting…just think of the peace and quiet you'll have. If you're not prepared to give them something to do that appeals to them, you'll give in and let them turn the TV on. ***But don't do it! This chapter is full of fun, educational activities that will keep children so busy for hours they won't even think of television again. But they have to be motivated! You can't just say, "Go Play," or "Go draw."***

Many very busy mothers may feel they don't have the time to help their kids get started on any of these activities, but ***if you just look through them you may find some that appeal to you and your child that you can fit into your schedule.***

You will need to purchase a scrapbook for your child from Walmart or any print store. A large one with sturdy covers and standard pages should cost under ten dollars and will last a long time. Make certain you can purchase extra pages. ***It must be kept for supervised projects. If you let the preschool child have it all the time, it will become tattered and she'll lose interest.***

To prevent the child from becoming bored, keep changing the activities. Some should be done with a parent, so be prepared to spend some time with your child, or skip them if you can't fit them into your busy schedule. You can set your younger child at the kitchen table while you're working in the kitchen and help her periodically. You may want to have more than one scrapbook for ongoing activities such as vocabulary words or alphabet activities. When the child loses interest, put the scrapbook away for a *rainy day.* You will need a lot of magazines and old books to cut up. Mail order catalogs are great. Look for used magazines at garage sales and bookstores. The activities that follow are enjoyable for children of all ages; just increase or decrease the difficulty to make them appropriate for your child's age:

Categorizing – Teach the child to categorize, compare, and organize pictures from magazines, catalogs, and newspapers. Give him a bunch of magazines from which to cut out pictures and paste them in the scrapbook. You can also use a cheap, lined, 3-hole notebook. Some topics may be:

> Foods – vegetables, fruit, dairy products, meat
> People – adults, boys, girls, babies, etc.
> Clothing – sports, work, dress-up, shoes, hats

Athletic Equipment – weights, balls, hockey, basketball
Community – buildings, churches, homes, schools
Living things – animals, insects, trees, plants

Sequencing – Read the newspaper cartoons to your child. Then cut them up, mix them up, and let your child paste them in proper sequence on each page. Do the same with comic books. The older child who can read will benefit from this activity after reading the cartoons herself, or before she reads them.

Colors – Help the preschool child learn the primary colors (red, blue, and yellow), and teach the school age child the secondary colors (green, orange, and purple). Write the name of the color on the top of each page and paste a sample next to it. Cut out numerous colored objects from old magazines and catalogs and let your child paste them on the corresponding pages.

Alphabet – For the child who's learning the ABC's, have her concentrate on one letter and sound at a time. Paste or print the letter being learned at the top of the page. Then fill up the page with letters cut from magazines and newspapers. If she's learning both the upper and lowercase letters, have her paste them side by side. You can also look together for pictures beginning with the letter. Keep this up with all the letters she's learning in school unless she gets bored with the activity. If she needs motivation, give stickers or stars for work well done.

Vocabulary – The word pairs listed below are synonyms, which are words that sound different but have the same meanings. One word in each pair is an easy one that school children already use. The other is a more sophisticated word that even some adults don't know. *When there is no television to watch*, the child would have more than enough time to enjoy drawing pictures depicting these words with written captions. For example, draw a picture of the family, even with stick figures, and a caption, "This is my *clan.*" A picture of stars and a caption, "Let's gaze at the stars." Draw the picture and write the caption on a piece of computer paper and tape it into the scrapbook. This may be an on-going project that she can add to whenever she needs something to do. You may prefer to use a 3-ring notebook for this project or a tablet. You will need to go over the words with the child so she can pronounce them. Encourage working together with friends or siblings.

excuse	alibi	fun	enjoyable
start	embark	ask	enquire

dry	arid	beg	plead
alone	isolated	dig	excavate
family	clan	hot	torrid
shout	bellow	busy	occupied
fang	tusk	mud	mire
odor	essence	ring	peal
fat	stout	thirsty	parched
stink	reek	zoo	menagerie
look	gaze	noise	uproar
storm	tempest	sharp	keen
warm	tepid	smell	whiff
trick	prank	thin	scrawny
speedy	rapid	corner	niche
home	abode	large	vast

Word Book – As the school-age child learns a new sight word, give her a small l" x 3" inch piece of tag board with the word printed on it, and let her paste it in the book. Or let her print the word in the book herself, and draw a picture to go with it, such as *banana, house,* or *snake.* Encourage her to use the word in a sentence. If the word is *stove,* the sentence could be, "Mommy cooks dinner on the stove." Print the sentence under the word and a picture of Mommy standing at the stove cooking, or just a picture of a stove. Encourage her to read her sentences to you. A ten- or twelve-year-old child's sentence could be, "The Tyrannosaurus Rex was a carnivorous animal." Give the child assistance, if needed.

Sight Words – When the child learns a sight word, write it on a small card l" x 3" and paste it onto a page. Fill the page with words she knows. Let her bring the book into the kitchen and sit at the table when you're cooking and say the words for you, or read her words to the family.

Book Record – When the early reader begins to read her own books, let her make an entry in the scrapbook for each book she completes. Print the name at the top of the page along with the illustrator and author. She can write it herself or dictate to you what she especially liked about the book, and then draw a picture to go with it. The older child will also enjoy keeping her own record.

Picture Sentences or Stories. – Cut interesting pictures from catalogs and magazines. Put them together to form a sentence using the pictures to fill in for words. For exam ple, if the child wants to use pictures of an ice cream cone and a puppy, a possible sentence could be, "The (paste in the picture of the puppy) wants to lick the little girl's (paste in the picture of the ice cream cone)."

Language Concepts – When the school-aged child learns nouns, pronouns, adjectives, quotations, or other language concepts, she can search magazines and newspapers for actual examples of the words, cut them out, and paste them in the scrapbook. This is a fun way to learn the words. For example, contractions are difficult for children to learn. Have her cut contractions from the newspapers and magazines, and paste them to a page. Next to each one she can print the two words they represent, such as *doesn't = does not.*

Vacation Reports – This activity would be for the eight-to fourteen-year-old child, and should be done in partnership with one of the parents. Before taking a vacation, help her write letters to the Chamber of Commerce of the state in which you will be traveling and request brochures about tourist attractions. While on the trip, the child may purchase postcards with pictures of scenes that particularly interest her. She could put these in her scrapbook along with any other photos, mementos, and written comments about the trip. When her scrapbook is filled, let her give a *Show and Tell* report to the family and grandparents about the family's vacation. Some teachers encourage students to give this type of report to the class.

Rather than write to the Chambers of Commerce, she could look up the location on the Internet and get similar information and pictures, but the cost of printing may be prohibitive. The experience in writing the letters and the excitement of receiving the mail may be preferred.

PART III

 SCHOOL SUCCESS

Chapter 22

SCHOOL BASICS

"You always pass failure on your way to success."

Mickey Rooney

Responsibility is the Backbone of Success

"If you want your children to be successful, you must teach them to take 100% responsibility for everything that affects them and everything they experience in their lives," says Jack Canfield in his classic, New York Times #1 best-selling book, *The Success Principles*, that has helped hundreds of thousands of people achieve success. In it, he stresses that *responsibility is the leading factor contributing to good grades, confidence, high self-esteem, independence, employability, and business success.*

By the time your children are ready to begin school, you should already have begun teaching them to assume responsibility for some of their personal needs, to clean up after themselves, and do minimal chores around the house, as outlined in Chapter 6, "Responsibility, The Key Ingredient of Success." You need to keep increasing these duties as they mature until, some day, they will be completely responsible for themselves and everything they experience. Personal and home responsibilities are prerequisites for children to be able to assume responsibility for their school related performances and learning. When your children finally enter school, your responsibilities will almost double. Following are the qualities which parents must assume to help them produce children who are top students:

Top Parents must:

- make education one of their family's top priorities.
- read to their children daily.
- praise and reward their children for effort and success.
- teach their children to be responsible for themselves.
- show their children how to benefit from their mistakes.
- make certain their children do their homework correctly and turn it in on time.
- teach their children to respect their teachers and obey school rules.

When children become students, their responsibilities will also nearly double; however, if their parents had already begun to give them responsibilities during their preschool years, they should be able to ease into their new school skills and learning with little effort. Following are the skills that must be part of top students' make-up:

Top Students must:

- have good attitudes.
- be motivated to learn.

- work up to their ability.
- ask for help when needed.
- turn their assignments in on time.
- learn from their mistakes.
- obey school rules.
- respect their teachers.

You will have a tough job ahead of you...years of patience, nagging, praising, encouragement, and consequences to reach your goal; most likely your child's entire school career from grades one through twelve. There will be times when you are too tired, have too many other responsibilities, and feel you just can't stretch any further; times when you're short of patience, when your kids are just impossible, and the best you can do is make them go to bed rather than fight with them to do what they're supposed to do. I can remember putting mine to bed and threatening them to not make a sound, not even ask for a drink of water; then I'd feel guilty because I was so mean to them. All this is a very normal part of being a good mother. ***Don't beat yourself up... you have a tremendous job to do! Just keep doing the best you can, day after day, and before you know it, you will be able to stand back and admire the results of all your hard work.***

This chapter is devoted to helping you organize your children's school days, from the time they get up in the morning until lights out after story time. All activities are based on training them to be responsible for their personal needs, school preparation, and learning. ***Keep in mind that feeling sorry for them and letting them sleep in, doing their chores for them, or helping them too much with their homework so they can watch a little television is not helping them, but will only delay their maturity and success. A good rule to follow is, "Don't do anything for your children that they can do for themselves."***

The Importance of Sleep

None of us can get along indefinitely without the amount of sleep our bodies consistently require. According to developmental experts, children need a healthy amount of sleep each night, as it directly affects their mental and physical growth. Most school days begin at 6:30 to 7:00 a.m., and end about 3:30 in the afternoon. Then after school activities, homework, and family matters may stretch children's days beyond their bedtimes, *especially when they are allowed to watch television.* **Without an average of ten** *to eleven hours of sleep each night children will end up with attention and retention problems, which affect their learning.*

During school days, children should have well-organized, consistent routines, whereby they have dinner at about the same time, do chores and homework, and prepare for their next school day. Only after these important things are done should the child have time for computer games or other entertainment, but these should never take the place of high quality contact time reading with a parent before lights out. School children should go to bed at night, and get up in the morning at the same time every day, just as adults do.

Importance of Physical Activity

Other than about fifteen minutes of recess and maybe twenty minutes of P.E. in school, children spend their entire day in a sedentary mode, quietly sitting at a desk, working with their minds. *When school is out, getting plenty of exercise in the forms of free play and sports is essential for them to continue their mental and physical development. Children should spend their time after school and before dinner running, climbing, riding bikes, rolling on the grass, romping with the dog, or any activity that makes them breathe hard and tires them out. Even if the weather is absolutely fierce outside, bundle them up and send them running around the block a few times.*

Routines

It's imperative to have daily routines, whereby the children do exactly the same thing every morning to get ready for school as well as well-planned routines for their after school, and evening activities; otherwise they'll waste time procrastinating, or doing unimportant things, and they'll never get important things done. *They must consistently do all that needs to be done, in 1-2-3 order, so the things they must do to get ready for school become habitual.* I would recommend that you list the activities on a chart, so you and your child can check each finished item and what needs to be done next.

You cannot expect first and second grade children to do everything themselves. You'll need to do most activities with them, gradually turning them over to do themselves. Nine-and ten-year-olds will be more efficient, but you will still need to do a lot of reminding to make sure they do what they're supposed to. You may even have to give consequences when they don't cooperate. *If you don't teach your children these routines, you will either have to do everything for them, or let them come to school*

disheveled, without homework and notes, probably without enough sleep. Here are some examples of routines:

Mornings

If you plan your child's time well the night before, as explained in "After Dinner" below, so that she puts her things away, prepares her book bag, and gets her clothes ready, then getting up and ready for school the following morning will run smoothly. The child needs to develop organized habits of what to do first, second, and so on that will blend in with what everyone else is doing. If you have a better schedule, use yours, but **understand that you must make plans with your children and follow them. You must practice with them and give them guidance.**

Before School

6:30 to 8:00 a.m.

- Get up with the alarm.
- Use the bathroom, wash up, comb hair.
- Get dressed in the clothes that were selected and set out the night before.
- Make the bed or pull sheets and blanket up to cover the mattress.
- Help mother pack lunch.
- Eat breakfast, clear off the table, and stack dishes in the washer or sink.
- Brush teeth.
- Put on jackets and outer wear, which should be in proper places.
- Gather school things which should have been prepared the night before.

If you don't plan, your mornings will be chaotic. I can remember looking frantically for shoes under beds, scattered schoolbooks, and for a jacket that had been left at school. And I'm sure the whole neighborhood grinned as I ran down the street after my kids, trying to beat the school bus with lunches in one hand, and a wet washcloth for dirty faces in the other. **This invariably happened to us when we didn't get ready the night before or get up with the alarm in the morning. Don't make the mistake of letting your child sleep in or not adequately preparing the night before.**

After School

3:30 to 5:00

- Snack (15 min)

- Empty school bag onto homework table. (5 min)
- Clean out lunch bucket and put it away. (5 min)
- Put notes and corrected papers in designated place for parent viewing. (1 min)
- Play outside or inside (1 hour)

Dinner

5:00 to 6:00

- Stop playing, put things away
- Put outdoor clothes in proper place.
- Wash up.
- Set the table.
- Eat dinner.
- Help clean up and load dishwasher

After Dinner

6:00 to 8:00

- Do Homework. Allow fifteen to sixty minutes from grades one to six.
- Organize backpack with books, lunch money, notes and supplies.
- Do art, reading, or other fun activities during extra time.
- Put personal belongings away.
- Set out clothes to wear the next day.
- Undress, put dirty clothes in the hamper.
- Put clean socks in shoes, ready to put on in the morning.
- Wash face and hands, brush teeth, and put on pajamas.
- Set dishes, silverware, and dry foods on the table for breakfast.
- Read a bedtime story from 8:00 to 8:30.
- Lights out no later than 8:30 for kids up to ten-years-old.

This looks like a lot, but other than homework, it shouldn't take more than thirty minutes to have everything ready before its time for the bedtime story at 8:00. ***When homework is completed, the book bag should be refilled with books, and everything needed for school the next morning.*** The outdoor clothes should always be in their proper place, ready to put on again. It's just a matter of organization, and seeing that the kids form habits to do what they're supposed to do, when they're supposed to, rather than have to do everything in panic at the last minute.

Backpacks

Every child looks forward to the purchase of his backpack with excitement. The styles get larger and more outlandish each year... with so many compartments and attachments, the child literally gets lost in them. Although meant to help him carry his school things, he will invariably stuff it with any of a number of other items that don't belong. *Backpacks, just like pants' pockets and purses, need to be cleaned out and reorganized daily. If not, they become the teachers' chief source of anguish and the students' frustration.*

Children's backpacks may be dangerously heavy, and could cause serious physical harm to the child carrying it. Recommended weight should not be more than 10% of the child's body weight. If you only get a back pack large enough for the essentials, then the child won't be tempted to put in shoes, baseballs, lunches, and other things that contribute to being over-weight.

With the use of a school backpack, it is the owners' responsibility to keep it clean and organized, but children don't automatically know how to do this... they must be taught how, just like any other skill. Because many parents do not teach this skill, a tremendous amount of stressful time is spent by teachers and students looking for items that can't be found. Small items like lunch money, notes, and pencils become buried among all the other things, and cannot be found unless the contents are completely dumped. Imagine several children having to dump their backpacks on the floor of the classroom or hallway in order to find what they need (no wonder many teachers have high blood pressure). Here are some examples of items I found in backpacks while trying to help my students find what they needed:

- cartons of sour milk
- moldy sandwich
- bits of candy
- broken pencils and crayons
- pencils and scattered shavings
- loose change
- dollar bills
- socks
- a tennis shoe
- overdue library books
- graded assignments not given to parents

- important notes not given to parents
- someone else's lost math book

I think you get the picture, but just in case…don't empty and organize your purse contents or clean out your car for two weeks and see what you'll find. ***The child should be taught how to clean and organize his backpack, and then be expected to completely empty it and clean it daily, preferably before he does his homework.*** Once she proves she can keep her backpack clean and organized, your daily inspection won't be necessary. The following items will facilitate organization:

- a small zipper bag in which to carry money
- a small zipper bag for pencils and eraser
- a small, portable pencil sharpener and a plastic zip-lock bag for shavings
- a flexible notebook in which to place paper

To simplify organization, have your child empty her backpack in this manner with you present giving guidance until she has developed the habit of doing it properly:

- Put books and homework items on the homework table.
- Put corrected assignments and notes in designated area for parents' viewing.
- Remove and sharpen pencils.
- Remove pencil sharpener shavings.
- Remove and discard unwanted items.

After homework has been completed and before bedtime, the backpack should be repacked for school the next day and placed in a designated area to be easily picked up on the way out the door. So you don't have to keep asking if she remembered each item, make a checklist of the things she should have in the bag and pin it to a convenient place. A poster board tacked on the wall next to the homework table would be ideal. Here's an example of such a checklist:

- lunch money
- school books
- notebook complete with clean papers
- sharpened pencils
- pencil sharpener and shavings bag
- envelope for take-home papers and notes
- signed notes to return to the teacher (if any)

This is a difficult habit for children to develop; however, it's very important and it is not too much to expect of them. Once they know how to clean, organize, and repack their backpacks, then they should be on their own, without nagging from mother. If they make a mistake and forget something, then let them face the consequences of not finding their homework, forgetting books, notes, or lunch money.

Incentives

Teaching children to do things for themselves can be tedious and boring. They'll rebel time and again when they have to do unpleasant things instead of play. They'll waste time, forget, or procrastinate. In the beginning, the most effective ways to get them to do as they're told are with hugs, kisses, and words of praise; however, many times you'll find yourself nagging, shouting, and punishing because they're uncooperative or forgetful. You need to decide which tasks your child should be expected to do without being told, or told more than once, and which ones are more difficult that will take more time to perform easily. Sit with your child and identify the behaviors he is expected to do and warn him of negative consequences (punishment) if he does not do them. For the behavior that is more difficult for him to perform consistently, discuss incentives that he can earn for effort and good performance.

Rewards – Either material rewards or extra privileges may be used, depending on your child's preference. They don't have to be lavish or given for every little accomplishment; in fact, the simpler you make them, the more effective they are. **Remember the philosophy that too much of something ruins a good thing. Keep your incentives special and sparse, and only for things the kids are having a difficult time learning or accomplishing,** such as doing a good job on their homework, getting ready for bed, or cleaning their bedroom. In this way, they'll try hard and have a good attitude, because they know they'll receive something special.

In the meantime, while the child is working toward learning and accomplishing in order to earn his reward, continue with the praise and words of encouragement, even when he makes a mistake. *Always* **praise the effort whether it leads to success or mistakes.**

To keep a record, give a sticker (or an x) on a calendar for each day the child does what is expected. When seven or more spaces are filled, she earns a predetermined reward. Make your own rules. Some rewards may require more effort. Here are suggestions for some simple, but enjoyable rewards:

- Pop popcorn and download a movie.
- Have a picnic at the park or in the back yard.
- Invite a friend over for pizza.
- Bake cookies with a friend.
- Trip to the zoo or park.
- Read an extra bedtime story.
- Spend special time with a parent.
- Stay up late on a Friday night.

Following are some responsibilities deserving of rewards that are very difficult to accomplish:

- Performing the morning routine is most important, because if the child doesn't follow hers properly, it can cause everyone to get off schedule, resulting in being late for school or work. It may take the first several weeks of each school year for the child to master this routine.

- Developing the homework habit is very difficult for children, usually until junior high. They can be restless and have difficulty sticking to the task, causing them to take too long or not get done at all. Some will procrastinate, play with their pencils, forget how to do the assignment, or have to use the restroom too many times.

- Getting ready for bed is always a challenge. Again, they will forget all that they need to do or take too much time to get everything done. They may take fifteen minutes to do what should take only five, which would take away from story-time. Getting things ready for the next morning is a great challenge and may take several weeks until habits are formed. A chart listing all the tasks would be very helpful, especially if you have her call out each item as she does it.

Sticker Charts – The old tried and true method of putting stars or stickers on calendars each time the child completes a difficult task or accomplishes a goal never fails. After so many stickers, he earns a reward or special privilege. This method is great for accomplishments that need to be developed over a period of time. By keeping the calendar in an obvious place, the child can determine his progress for himself. Here are just a few difficulties the child needs help to overcome:

- getting up and ready for school in the morning
- sitting still to complete homework

- keeping bedroom clean and orderly
- keeping bedroom, drawers and closets clean and organized
- breaking a bad habit

Clock Timers – A timer is a great motivator. Set it for a reasonable time and challenge the child to **beat the clock.** Rewards may not be necessary... just the excitement of finishing the task could be enough to get her to do the following tasks in record time:

- doing chores
- getting ready for bed and story time
- getting clothes and school things ready for the next morning
- doing the morning routine
- completing homework

Negative Consequences

- early bedtime
- no television on weekends
- having to spend time in his room
- extra chores
- loss of favorite privileges
- time out
- loss of time with parent
- loss of play time

Children need both positive and negative consequences to help shape their behavior; either one, when used exclusively, will fail in encouraging the desired behavior and preventing the bad.

Incentives are intended to help the young child stick to the task, or develop hard-to-remember routines without having to be nagged or punished. When the child demonstrates that he is capable of performing his responsibilities, incentives should be discontinued and the desired behavior should be expected. If he regresses, then negative consequences should be given again.

Chapter 23

HOME-SCHOOL COMMUNICATION

"Communication Works for those who Work at it."

John Powel

Parent/Administration

When your child begins school, you'll want to know how he's doing, long before report cards and teachers' conferences: what's happening in his classroom, what he's being taught, does he need help, what is expected of him, and what he has for homework. It's never a good excuse to say, "I don't know what my child needs help with," or "I didn't know he was failing." *It's your responsibility to find these things out, without calling the teacher every day or week. But how can you do this?*

First, you must acquaint yourself with the school, its principal, and your child's teacher. Begin every school year by attending the school's Open House, which is usually held about a month after school begins. At this time, most teachers will tell parents how they conduct their classes, give a brief outline of the skills and concepts they will be teaching, and what they expect of their students.

From here on, attend all of the PTA meetings to show your interest and support, and if you are a work-at-home mom and have the time, offer the teacher your assistance. Teachers always need help and are grateful for even the slightest, especially listening to the students read. In my particular case, besides always needing help listening to individual students read, I needed help in my art classes, because there were so many students, and it took so long to clean up. When I didn't have help, the classes had to be shorter, so I couldn't spend as much time with my students as I would have liked.

You might even request permission to sit in on one of your child's classes so you can observe him and the class routine. This could be done while you're listening to other children read. It would be interesting for you to stay the entire day, if allowed.

Your child's teacher will most likely call you if your child has a major problem; he may even have a system set up whereby you can communicate with emails. Otherwise, if you want to keep up on your child's progress, and don't want to wait for monthly grade reports or semester conferences, *you are going to have to rely on your child to be the middle person, the one who will carry information from school to home. You will need to train him, but it will be worth the effort if you really want to know what is happening in school.*

Parent/Child/School Communication

The first and most important step in communicating is showing an interest in what your child is doing in school. *If you always talk about what he's learning with excite ment and enthusiasm, he'll rush home from school every day, bursting with news about what he did. In the eyes of a child, getting his parents' approval is the most wonderful thing that can happen to him. If you act interested, listen, and ask questions each time he tells you about his day, he will go to school with a mind-set to listen for something you may want to hear about.* This desire for your approval will start him on the road to being a good student, because it will encourage him to be more alert and pay better attention.

- At first, the events he'll tell you about will seem trivial: what he did for recess, with whom he played or sat for lunch. You should be interested in these activities, because good social skills are a very important part of his self-esteem. At these times you can encourage development of kindness, fairness, and friendships. Also be one-up on bullying or know if he doesn't have any friends, both of which would warrant a special conference with his teacher.

- An older child will be able to tell you his class routines…what class he has first or second and which ones are before and after lunch. You should know when the students are allowed to sharpen pencils and use the restroom, when they are allowed to talk, and when they must be silent. All this information gives you an idea of the classroom atmosphere and rules, so you may discuss them with your child.

- Encourage your child to participate in class by volunteering to read and to ask questions. Because he knows he will be pleasing you, he will go out of his way to be active in class. Consequently, he will be much more outgoing and a better student. Ask him each day if he raised his hand to ask or answer any questions. Praise him if he did, and if he didn't, encourage him to do so the next opportunity.

- You can set his mind by telling him you want to know about things in specific subjects. For example, you might ask, "What did you learn in Math today?" "What story did you read?" "Did you learn any new vocabulary words today?" "Did you play any games?" "What would you like to tell me about your day?" "Did your teacher listen to you read?"

- Try to develop an open line of communication with your child, so he will even feel comfortable telling you about times when he was reprimanded or didn't know the answer to a question. Ask him if he was good all day or if he got

- in trouble. What trouble did he get into or did someone else get in trouble? Refrain from acting disappointed or chastising him, because that will be the last time he'll tell you about the negative side of his school life.

- Get into a daily talk time habit. Take turns telling each other something about your days. Be interested with each activity he shares with you. Relate an experience you had that would be especially interesting to him. Tell your child often that you are proud of him.

Student Assignments

Usually, verbal communication with your early grade child and viewing his corrected assignments will tell parents much of what they need to know. As students advance to higher grades they will be given assignments in more than one subject, such as to read a certain number of pages in their reader, work problems two through fifteen on page twenty-seven in Math, and answer the questions after chapter ten in Social Studies. Most teachers try to help the students keep track of their assignments. If this is the case, reinforce their system from home. *Otherwise, you need to help your child take notes to remind him of what he has for homework.*

I often wished that parents could observe their child in the classroom. They would be enlightened as to why their child consistently forgets his books or what he had for homework. In my room I would verbally give the assignments and then write them on the chalkboard. The lessons were added each time we completed another subject, and they were left on the board until the next day. The problems some of my students encountered were enough to frustrate me as well.

Here are just a few:

- They couldn't find the tablet on which to write their assignments.
- They couldn't find a pencil.
- They lost their notes when it was time to go home.

Children should not be punished for forgetting their homework until they've been helped to develop habits that will help them to remember or how to efficiently take notes. By second grade, the child should be able to write down his assignments. Following is a never-fail method that you can teach your child:

- Give him a sheet of wide-lined notebook paper to fold and keep as a marker in *each book.* When the teacher teaches a lesson from any particular book,

- and gives an assignment, the child is to jot it down on the marker in that book. There should be no need to write complete sentences, just page numbers and perhaps one or two words to explain the assignment. Keep the same paper as a marker in the same book. This method is so simple, every child should be able to follow it.

- Usually the teacher will teach a lesson and then give an assignment for the students to do in class and complete for homework if they don't finish. These notes will give you some insight. If the child seldom has homework you can insist that he bring each book home and tell you what he did that day and have him show you his bookmark indicating what he was assigned. Bringing home all the books together would be too heavy so try just one or two at a time. Tell him in the morning that you want him to bring home a particular book, such as Math. When he does, see what he has written on the bookmark. Have him bring home a different book the next day, and so on. His teacher may assign homework differently. If so, find out so you know how to train your child.

If he says he completes his assignments in class, have him bring them home each day to show you. You can discontinue this after a while when you're certain that he is doing his work. At this time you can check his work for accuracy and neatness. If he's being careless, you can have him do it over. If you see his work before he turns it in, then you'll know ahead of time what to expect when he gets it back, corrected, from his teacher.

The bookmark for homework assignments will work until the child reaches middle grades. Then he'll be ready for a commercial planner made for school children in which to keep notes for homework assignments as well as other things such as softball games, music lessons, or other responsibilities. You should not have to check on your child in this manner indefinitely; just for a few months, until he has developed the good habits of remembering his homework and working according to your expectations. When this happens, periodic parent/teacher conferences scheduled by the school should be sufficient to talk to your child's teacher about his progress, and any problems you may need to help him with at home. If you find that he has problems that you weren't aware of, then you should go back to checking on his work daily again.

Chapter 24

VIEWING CORRECTED ASSIGNMENTS

"When adults realize that every human being – especially the adolescent – hungers for understanding, acceptance, and recognition, many of the problems of delinquency will be on their way to solution."

William A. Ward

The best way of knowing your child's progress is from the assignments he does in ***class or for homework.*** The teacher checks them for correctness or errors, gives them a grade, and returns them to the child to take home to his parents. If the child gets good grades with very few errors, he'll skip happily home and present you with his papers marked with stars and A's and B's. You'll no doubt hug him and praise him for doing so well, but when he brings home papers with a lot of checkmarks and bad grades, you'll know that he needs help.

But suppose your child never brings his graded papers home? If he doesn't, then you won't know how he's doing until report cards come out, which is too late to get him the help he needs.

Why Some Students Don't Bring Their Corrected Assignments Home.

There's one problem that seems universal among the parents of students who usually don't do well. They never get to see their children's corrected assignments. The first thing these parents would ask me during conferences is why they never get their child's corrected papers. Their child's excuses were anywhere from, "The wind blew them away," "They were left on the bus," or "The teacher never gives any papers back."

I did everything I could from a teacher's standpoint to get my students to take their papers home. I gave them each a folder in which to place their papers. I would accumulate several, then pass them out all together right before dismissal. They were to put them in their folder and take it home to their parents. Can you imagine my frustration when parents would come to conferences and say, "Why don't we ever get any corrected papers? My child tells me you never give back his papers." Why do some children take their papers home for parents' approval while others do not? Let's look into some possible answers:

- They are ashamed of their mistakes.
- They get scolded and punished for making mistakes.
- Mommy and Daddy are upset when they don't get A's.
- Their parents don't look at their papers.
- They don't turn in their assignments, so they don't have papers to bring home.

When the parents scold and punish the child for getting poor grades, his feelings of ***inadequacy and failure are reinforced, and he begins to hide his papers, or conveni-*** ***ently lose them, so his parents won't see them. He'll even resort to lying in order to*** ***keep from getting into trouble.***

How Can You Get Your Child to Bring His Papers Home?

It isn't easy. In the first place, if you show anger or disappointment, and threaten your child with punishment if he doesn't do better, then forget it. *No child is going to skip happily home to give Mommy and Daddy his papers marked up with check marks and D's and F's, when they'll be met with scolding and punishment for not doing better.* Instead, show an interest in his papers by sitting down with him to look at them together.

When the child's school papers indicate he's having trouble understanding the assignment, the parents must be willing to help him at home. Keep in mind that there may be twenty to thirty students in your child's class. Most teachers will go out of their way to give children extra help, and parents should encourage their child to ask for it. But many children need more one-on-one assistance than teachers can give them. *The time a child receives in assistance from his parents is invaluable. No teacher can match it.*

If parents don't make themselves available, the child may get too far behind to get caught up. Each time a new lesson is explained that is contingent upon understanding the prior one, his situation becomes even more hopeless. Your first challenge will be to get him to bring each and every one of his corrected papers home to you. These will give you almost immediate knowledge of his needs, rather than having to wait for report cards or conferences. The following guideline should help you:

- The first thing you need to do is have a conference with your child's teacher and have your child with you. Find out any problems he may have and ask for the teacher's advice.

- Make it clear to your child that you love him, and want him to do well in school. Tell him he is very bright and capable of getting good grades, but he needs to ask his teacher or you for help when he doesn't understand. Assure him that making mistakes is part of learning, and that when he gets poor grades its only because he doesn't understand or didn't try hard enough.

- Give him a special folder in which to place the papers to be brought home. This could simply be a large manila envelope that can be folded over to fit into his backpack. This is the first step in stressing the value of his completed, corrected work.

- Expect him to bring his papers home to you whenever he receives them from

- the teacher. Help him develop the habit of bringing this folder home daily, whether it contains papers or is empty. This way it should never be forgotten.

- Discuss consequences if he doesn't bring the folder home or hides his papers. He may be forgetting it deliberately, because he is getting bad grades, or is not turning in his assignments.

Viewing the Child's Corrected Assignments

Always find the time to look at your child's papers. If possible, do this each time he brings one home. If your schedule doesn't allow for the time, provide a basket or box in which to put the papers. Then on weekends, after dinner, or *as soon as you can,* sit down with your child and examine his work together.

- Tell her often that she's just as smart as anyone else, but just needs to know how to learn. Look at a paper that is well done, and use it as proof that she can do good work. Make positive comments about how well he does.

- Emphasize the importance of learning from his mistakes!

- Know your child's potential! Don't be critical of poor handwriting, sloppy work, or many mistakes if the child is doing the best he can. Neat work comes with practice.

- Look for improvement or something to praise! If the child is showing carelessness, discuss this as well as the good work End the session with a big hug and tell him you are looking forward to the better work you know he is capable of doing. Then watch for the slightest improvement, so that you can make a big to do about it: "See there! I knew you could do it! I'm very proud of you. You're very smart and capable. This is good work."

- Teach him to be proud of his work and to be his own critic. In this way, he will grow to be self-motivated and strive for good grades for his own satisfaction, a much deeper gratification than praise and rewards from you.

- Decide together which papers are great, which ones show the most improvement, and which ones were done carelessly.

- If a paper is particularly poor, let him help you find the reason. Was he having a bad day when the assignment was given? Was he daydreaming? Did he not understand the concept. Did he raise his hand and ask the teacher questions or

- ask for help? Did he ask you for help? If he was careless, he should understand the consequences are having to do it over.

Dealing with Mistakes

Making mistakes is a normal part of growing up and daily living, but there must be a lesson learned each time we make one. A person must profit from the discomfort, pain, or inconvenience caused by the mistake, or he will continue to make the same one over and over. Most adults have serious hang-ups about making mistakes. Take yourself for instance. How do you feel when you make a mistake? Are you ashamed to admit it? Do you chastise yourself, thinking, "How could I have done such a stupid thing? Do you make excuses about what caused you to do something incorrectly? I would venture to say that a good amount of adults feel this way at times when they make a mistake.

If no one is perfect, and making mistakes is such a normal part of living, why do people have such a fear of doing something wrong, and how do they get that way? Let's go all the way back to early childhood and our school years. The child is constantly scolded and punished for making mistakes: breaking things, spilling milk, getting dirty, making too much noise, and so on. When he goes to school, he makes more mistakes. He's constantly reprimanded by his parents for doing something wrong. Amid all these bad things, he does a lot of nice things, too, but unfortunately, he doesn't get praised for these things. He only remembers the scolding and punishments he gets for making mistakes.

Consequently, the child grows up fearful of doing something wrong and making mistakes. When he does, he'll do anything to keep others from knowing, because they'll think he's bad, dumb, not good enough, incapable, or not qualified.

You can prevent your child from being swallowed up by this dilemma by helping him to see himself as a normal person who is continually in the process of learning through making mistakes. Call attention to the fact that you and everyone else makes mistakes. Don't let him think that you are only proud of him when he doesn't make any mistakes. *Whether your child is an A or an F student, you must let him know that you are proud of him and love him.*

Throughout daily contact with your family, make it a point to discuss, without shame or blame, mistakes as they occur and how each of you will learn from them. Let your child see how you are penalized by your own mistakes, and point out to him the les sons you have learned. Tell him stories about the times you made mistakes in your past that caused you hardships, for example: the speeding ticket and the fine you had to pay; forgetting about something cooking on the stove and the cleaning up you had to do; the time you forgot to make the house mortgage payment and had to pay the overdue charges; or the time you forgot to turn off the hose and had a huge water bill to pay. Discuss Grandma's and Grandpa's wisdom, which they gained from living so long and learning from their mistakes. My students were very impressed when I told them how I forgot to put gas in my car and was late for work, or the time I was driving too fast and got a ticket and had to pay a fine. ***Knowing that making mistakes is a part of living will help children accept themselves and the mistakes they have made and will make.***

Learning From Mistakes

If the child makes a lot of mistakes and gets a few correct, have him do a few over with you present so you know he understands the process. Then have him correct the others himself. Assure him that all he needs to do is check his work for mistakes, ask for help with understanding if he needs it, and then correct them. ***Then encourage him to always proofread his work in order to get a good grade. Praise him for his effort and pin his corrected paper on the wall of pride.***

- When the child has worked hard proofreading on her own, but still has a few mistakes, don't make her go back and proofread again. Just praise her work and tell her that the more she tries, the better she will get, and she will. On the other hand, if she continues to struggle and makes many errors when you know she is trying her best, ask the teacher to have her tested for learning disabilities.

- Once you know your child's capabilities, insist that she work up to them and proofread on her own. If she's making too many mistakes and you know she can do better, then you need to find out why. Some common reasons are carelessness or lack of understanding.

- Carelessness should not be accepted, and the penalty should be to do the assignment over, because she didn't do it correctly the first time. If the child did not understand the explanation, then it is her responsibility to ask the teacher for more help. If she didn't, and consequently didn't do the assignment correctly, then the penalty should be to have to do it over when she does understand it. In this way, the child learns from her mistakes of being careless and not asking questions when she doesn't understand an assignment.

When it comes to critiquing your child's work, always let it be accompanied with a warm hug. In case you might be afraid of sounding like a broken record, here are a number of ways to express your approval or react in a positive way toward good or unsatisfactory work your child gives you:

- "You must be proud of these papers!"
- "You're doing great!"
- "I love the colors you use!"
- "I like your handwriting!"
- "I can tell you like school. Look at the beautiful work you do!"
- "I would love to hear your story. Please read it to me."
- "Maybe you're going to be a famous author when you grow up."
- "You're becoming a real math whiz!"
- "You're getting better."
- "You're improving because you try so hard."
- "I'm very proud of you for trying so hard."
- "Keep up the good work."

Encouragement

- "It's okay to make mistakes. That's how we learn."
- "If we never made mistakes, then how would we ever get better?"
- "Wow! You made a lot of mistakes. Did you understand the assignment?"
- "Did you ask the teacher for more help?"
- "The only time I'll scold you is when you're careless or don't ask for help when you need it."
- "Oh Jimmy, you made way too many mistakes. There's a problem somewhere. Here, let's sit down and work some of these together. I'm sure you'll do better once you understand."
- "When you make this many mistakes it means only one thing… you didn't understand how to do the assignment. Many students don't understand an explanation the first time, but it's their responsibility to ask questions until they do."
- "Did you know that smart people ask the most questions? That's how they learn to get the answers."
- "I'm proud of you for trying so hard. I know it's frustrating to work so hard and still make so many mistakes, but if you don't find out what you did wrong and correct your mistakes, you won't learn."
- "I watched you do your lesson, and you were in a hurry and didn't proofread

- your work. Let's see how many you got wrong that you could have gotten correct if you put more effort into it. Always remember, the harder you try, the
better you get."

Displaying Papers

Display school papers on a wall designated for drawings, stories, and corrected papers.
I used my kitchen wall where we could look at them while we ate our meals and discuss
them together. Emphasize the papers he did over and the mistakes he corrected. This
will fill the child with pride and motivate him to continue to do well and to improve.

*Your child's corrected assignments are records of his school success or failure. If he
gets poor grades, he has problems that he needs help with. Parents must work with
the teachers to get him on track.*

Chapter 25

HOMEWORK

"Perhaps the most valuable result of all education is the ability to make your-self do the thing you have to do, when it ought to be done, whether you like it or not; it is the first lesson that ought to be learned; and however early a man's training begins, it is probably the last lesson that he learns thoroughly."

Thomas Henry Huxley

Homework is a hassle, but like it or not, both parents and students must accept it as a major part of the child's education. The essential reasons for a student having homework assignments are to:

1. Practice and reinforce the skills they were taught in class.
2. Help teachers to recognize how well their students understand the concepts.
3. Provide parents with the opportunity to become involved in their child's schoolwork.
4. Help students learn time management, responsibility, and organization,

It's important for parents to understand that children are not born with good homework skills…they need help to develop them, just as they need help learning to load the dishwasher and clean their rooms. It's the parents' job to provide the child with the guidance he needs, so he can become a responsible and self-reliant student. *Unfortunately, there are no established methods that teach parents how much to help their child, or when not to help him. That is why homework continues to be a major concern of education.*

Helping the child with homework doesn't mean telling him the answers, or doing the work for him; rather it is to provide the right environment and time in which to do it, along with specific guidelines that will lead to homework independence, which I will provide in this chapter.

Atmosphere

The impact of music on effective studying is debatable. Most children insist that they cannot study without their music, while parents maintain that because music bothers them when they're trying to read, then it undoubtedly must bother their children. *Research clearly indicates that loud music and television prevent accuracy while studying, and that students learn more in a quiet atmosphere.* Solve the problem by starting the young learner out by studying while it's quiet. When the child is older, let him experiment with music in the background. As a compromise, allow him to listen to soft background music.

Keep in mind that when there are several members of a family, all involved in different activities, such as television, loud music, laughing and talking, it would be very difficult for a child to attempt to concentrate on homework. An hour of quiet time scheduled consistently each evening is worth considering for the entire family, if that's possible. Parents can read, write out bills, or be on hand to help the children with their homework. If busy parents need to do other things during this time, they should try to restrict talking and making noise. *The television and music should be off for the study hour; however, if this is an impossibility, at least have the participant use earphones or have the child's study place far enough away from the TV that it won't distract him.*

Time and Place

The message should be clear that in your home, schoolwork is one of the first priorities. Fun activities such as artwork, playing games, computer games, or even going shopping with a parent should be scheduled *after* homework is completed. I prefer to let the younger child play outside after school and do homework after dinner. Be flexible with the older child in the case of after-school activities, such as ball games or scout meetings; however, if the outside activities interfere with homework, then they should be discontinued.

Although many older students prefer to do their homework in what seems the most illogical places, *the younger students' time and area should be structured. Good study habits are conducive to effective studying and good grades. The time to begin developing good homework habits is when the child first begins to receive homework assignments.* Teachers' assignments vary from about fifteen minutes for younger students to one hour for fifth and sixth grade students.

Ask the child's teacher if you should expect your child to have homework every night. If your child never has any, find out why. If she gets all her work done in class, ask the teacher to give her extra activity work to do at home. Children should have homework each night, with some exceptions. This time should be designated as quiet time and there should be no drinks, phone calls, snacks, or television.

If they have no homework, it may be a good idea to have them bring their work home to proofread. In this way you'll get a good idea of the work they do in school. You might consider allowing your child to select a scrapbook or writing activity mentioned in this book to do during this period. Television viewing should not be allowed in place of reading or some other creative, enjoyable activity.

The favorite homework place in my family when my three kids were little was at the kitchen table where I could keep busy with things in the kitchen and be available to help them when they needed me. *I was also able to observe them, to look over their shoulder, and make sure they knew what they were doing.* In this way they were all together, so I didn't have to go traipsing back and forth from room to room. The des ignated time was one hour. Those who finished early could do art work, hobbies, or get ready for bed.

Parents' Involvement

Children love the attention and extra help they can get from parents and will get as much of it as they can by asking for more help than they should have. They'll play on the parents' sympathy by feigning confusion and tears, claiming they can't do the work. They'll nag and pester until the parents give in and spend more time than should be required to help the child. ***Parents must be cautious not to allow a too dependent relationship to occur which will prevent the child from ever developing confidence in her own ability.***

The Child's Responsibility

When the child first enters school, parents should make it clear that it is her responsibility to pay attention, and make certain that she understands what is being taught. If she doesn't understand, the first person she should ask for assistance is the teacher. This may start out by being very difficult for the shy child, but this problem must be overcome. In cases where the child is just too fearful to ask, the parent should make the teacher aware of the child's problem. A special conference with the parent, child, and teacher may make the child feel more comfortable when asking for help. In my classroom, the shy children felt comfortable holding up one finger under their chin or in front of their chest, indicating that they didn't understand. I would go to the child's desk to give personal assistance. ***Confident children raise their hands and ask questions freely, without fear of appearing dumb, which is something you should help your child strive to achieve.***

Homework Routine

First you must develop a plan to help the child remember what her homework is, and which books to bring home. A very simple way of keeping track of homework is to keep a folded notebook paper in each book as a bookmark. Each time the teacher gives an assignment, the child can jot down the page number and items to be done. This should be a foolproof method of knowing what the homework assignment is.

Before the child begins, have her empty her schoolbag of all items needed. Have the homework table cleared of everything not needed for homework. A kitchen table filled with dinner dishes, ketchup, newspapers, or other items is very distracting to a child attempting to concentrate. Follow this procedure if the assignment is Math:

- Ask the child what she has for homework. All she should have to do is resort to the bookmark in order to know. Have her read the directions and then watch her to see if she does one or two items correctly. If she does them correctly, leave her alone while she completes the assignment.

- If she does the first item wrong, have her read the directions again and tell you what they tell her to do. If she still needs help show her how and have her do the next two herself while you observe. If you're convinced she knows how, leave her alone to complete the assignment.

- Have her bring her completed assignment to you. If it's messy and you know she can do a better job have her do it over. If she was careless and has made too many mistakes, point out her mistakes and have her do the assignment over.

- Know your child's capabilities. Beginning students are usually messy. They don't form their letters well and have to erase often. Emphasize neatness, but don't insist on perfection; however, do insist on her best work. If you observe her rushing through the assignment and not taking time to be neat then you should have her do it over.

- If your elementary school child is responsible, has average ability, and works hard on her homework, but consistently needs more than an hour to complete it, you should call the teacher to see if there's a problem. Sometimes teachers will assign too much, but you may find out that your child isn't using her time well in class, and consequently has more homework than she should have.

- Strongly emphasize proofreading. Work one problem, then do it again to see if she got the same answer. If not, then she should re-read the directions and work the problem again until she gets the same answer twice.

- Once your child knows the homework routine, you should let her work independently. If she brings home papers with many errors, you will know that she's either being careless, not proofreading, or not asking for help when she doesn't understand the assignment. Either way, she is responsible and should have to pay the consequences of having to correct the errors at a time when she could be having fun doing something else.

Teach your child to always read the directions more than once and to proofread his work, whether the assignment is in Language, Social Studies, Spelling or Math. Mistakes are easy to make and the students who go back to look for them and correct them are the ones who get the best grades.

Timer

A clock or timer is the most valuable tool a parent can have when helping the child develop self-discipline and good homework habits. *It's also excellent for assisting the slow child to speed up his effort, or for the child who has difficulty sitting for any length of time to complete the homework tasks.* Begin with short sessions, ten to fifteen minutes, and build up to a half hour. The child must sit and work hard until the timer goes off. Allow a bathroom break and start again until the task is completed. When the habits are formed, and the child can reliably sit for the amount of time necessary to complete his work, then the clock is no longer necessary. If you have an obstinate child who refuses to sit still and work, even though he knows how, then you may have to give him a choice of cooperating or going to bed.

Once the child becomes independent and expected to do his homework properly, he should be left alone to do it. *If he plays around, procrastinates, and doesn't get it done before bedtime, he should go to bed regardless and suffer the consequences of not having his homework done. He shouldn't be nagged or enticed.*

If you are consistent the first several weeks of each grade in helping your child develop these homework skills and habits, she will gradually achieve homework independence with minimal help from you; *however, if your elementary school child is responsible, working at average or below level, and works hard on her homework, but consistently needs help, consider that she may have a learning disability and ask the school to have her evaluated. Keep in close contact with her teacher and counselor for feedback and advice.*

Chapter 26

SOCIAL PROBLEMS

"Life is too short for hate and not long enough for love."

George Peppard

Social difficulties in children form as soon as peer interaction begins, some as early as preschool, becoming more advanced in grade school and much more severe in high school. ***When children enter school, making friends and becoming accepted is a very important part of their lives; however, it's not all about having fun and making friends. With socializing comes hurt feelings when they lose a best friend, when they're ridiculed, left out of social events, or ousted from a group.*** According to findings published in the April 2018 issue of the *Journal of Developmental and Behavioral Pediatrics,* nine out of ten elementary school kids have been subjected to physical or psychological bullying by their peers.

In the early grades bullying is usually in the form of ridicule and teasing. ***A child may be victimized for any number of reasons, perhaps because of the shoes she wears, or maybe because she's smarter than the other students, overweight, or disliked because she's athletic. A boy might be ridiculed because he's clumsy, always strikes out when playing ball, is smaller than the others, or is just shy and a loner.*** Unkind children will invariably find something to point to and laugh at. In my case, when I was in 5th grade, because I was taller than all of the other students, they called me "string bean," "skinny," and "spider legs." I had no one to turn to who could assure me that although everyone is different from each other, everyone is still beautiful.

The effects of bullying can be severe and long lasting. I began to see myself as ugly, awkward, and too large. I developed feelings of inferiority and a low self-concept which followed me well into adulthood.

Both genders take part in bullying, although in different forms. Older girls usually form social groups with other girls and will gossip, criticize, or ridicule those not in their group. Or their leader may direct attention to another girl in the group that may seem a threat to her leadership position and all the others will shun her. Boys tend to be more physically aggressive and impulsive and will attack and start fights with other boys who show shyness or weakness. They, too, form groups of followers who are looking for acceptance. The followers will often do anything or say anything, just to maintain their position within the group. Bullying in grade school is relatively mild until about 6th grade, closer to junior high when students begin using smartphones. Then it becomes quite brutal. ***Parents should be knowledgeable about social problems and prepared to help their child through them, because it will very likely happen to him or her and will get much worse the older the child gets.***

What Makes A Bully?

Bullies and their followers seem to enjoy hurting others, but in reality, they have severe problems and don't know how to help themselves. There are a number of factors that cause children to become bullies, *chief among them is modeling their parents' behavior.* Perhaps they're abused by their parents or older siblings, or witness their parents abusing each other; they may hear them use bad language when talking about others or speak critically of neighbors, relatives, or friends. They may hear their parents berate a sales clerk, make irate phone calls to complain about something, or cuss out another car driver.

These children may either receive very harsh discipline or none at all, while their home entertainment consists of constant viewing of violent television, movies, and computer games. *All these behaviors exhibited within the home give children the message that its o.k. to humiliate someone, say mean things about them, or make them feel bad.*

If your child's teacher tells you that your child is showing hurtful or aggressive tendencies, you need to observe his/her behavior and watch for warning signs, such as anger, jealousy, hate, or constant criticisms that would indicate that your child needs help. You need to have the courage to examine your own behavior, and if your child's behavior is a result of what he sees and hears you do, if you really care about him, you must diligently work on changing the atmosphere of your home and your own behavior. *Recent studies indicate that some children who are bullies while in school, often grow up to be criminals when they become adults. Seek help from a school counselor and professional counseling, if necessary.*

Not all bullying is the result of parent modeling; some unkind children may just be insecure and critical of themselves. Finding faults in others seems to make them feel better. Other causes of bullying are a lack of empathy, or not having the ability to imagine, or understand the hurt that someone else feels, which may lead a child to treat others unkindly.

Dealing With Bullies

Open communication within a family is extremely important. Family members should be comfortable talking about and sharing things that happen to them in their daily lives, how they feel about things, and their likes and dislikes. Parents should encourage their children to come to them about anything that concerns them, good or bad, even if they got in trouble in school. In order to get their children's trust, if their child confides in them, parents must never criticize or scold their child if it's something he did wrong. If they discuss the child's concerns or wrongdoings in a kind and loving manner, when he needs support and someone to talk to when he gets in trouble, or is approached by bullies in school, he won't be embarrassed or afraid to come to his parents for help.

It is important that when children approach parents with social problems, parents stop what they're doing and take the time to listen and ask questions. Discuss the problem and possible solutions. If you over-react and become angry with the bullies and threaten to call their parents, your child may become fearful that he'll be called a tattle tale and things will get worse. Consequently, he may never confide in you again. First, consider helping the child solve the problem himself by trying the following:

- Try to befriend the bully.
- Ignore the bad treatment.
- Avoid the bully.
- Walk away from the bully.
- Find other friends.
- Join another group.

Be An Involved Parent

It's not enough to know about your child's school life and friends. Parents need to go further and know about other people who are part of their child's life. Some ways to do this include:

- Participate in parent/school organizations.
- Be close to your child's teacher.
- Volunteer to spend time helping your child's teacher.
- Know who your child's friends are.
- Make certain your child has desirable friends.
- Know the parents of your child's close friends.
- Volunteer to take your child and friends to social events.
- Ask your child about her day: assemblies, friends, playground activities.
- Ask your child about bullying in school, who is bullied, and why.
- If possible, befriend the parents of the bullies.
- Be involved in your child's school bully prevention program.

Although children must learn to solve their own problems, and learn to stand up for themselves, parents can do a lot to help them reach that point. When bullying first begins, it will be helpful to tell your child that the unkind child has problems that are making her very unhappy; perhaps she's being abused, or she may not feel good about herself. In many cases, this is true. If a socially abused child understands this, she may be spared from thinking that something is wrong with her

Teaching Kindness and Empathy

Kindness is a trait that must be instilled at home; unfortunately, many parents take this ability for granted; *they don't realize that if they don't teach their children to be kind, they will learn to be cruel from their peers in school. This is almost a certainty. If you don't want your child to be cruel and hurtful to others, then you must go out of your way to teach her or him to be kind and sensitive to the feelings of others. Following are behaviors parents should incorporate into their parent/child relationship and training.*

- If you're having a birthday party for your child, invite the entire class, girls or boys, or just a few close friends. Explain to your child how hurtful it is to be uninvited.
- When sending out valentines, always give a valentine to every child in class. Help your child understand how hurtful it would be not to receive valentines from everyone.
- Send cake and punch to school for the entire class to celebrate your child's birthday.
- Teach your child to reject gossip about another child. Discuss unkind conversations about other people. Give actual examples by role-playing.
- Ask your child how she would feel being the object of gossip and unkind remarks.
- Never laugh at the mistakes of another student in class.
- Encourage your child to befriend someone that is shy and has no friends.
- Encourage your child to sit with someone who has no one to sit with when having lunch.
- Find something nice to say to another child, especially one who isn't very popular.
- Encourage your child to befriend a disabled child, or one who has disfiguring characteristics.
- Never laugh at or ridicule a person who is different, such as one who is overweight, clumsy, gets poor grades, dresses differently or is different in some way.
- Be a friend to classmates who are different and include them in activities.

- In general, teach your child to always treat others as she would like to be treated.
- Coach your child in stopping the bullying of another child, such as shouting "STOP," or telling a teacher.

Psychiatrists will tell you that unkind people have problems of their own which cause them to act in negative ways. By allowing an unkind person to hurt you, you are permitting that person to control your life by making you unhappy. The abused child needs to be helped to feel empathy for the bully. ***Discuss with your child some of the problems the bully may have, such as a poor home life, physical and verbal abuse at home, and parental neglect. This philosophy should be combined with kindness toward the child's abuser, instead of anger. This may be difficult, but in the long run, it helps the abused child avoid becoming hurt and withdrawn and helps them to develop empathy for unhappy and troublesome people. It may even lead to friendship.***

Harmless Teasing

Many times children mean no harm, and just get a bang out of teasing others, not realizing they are being hurtful. For example, one child in my classroom, Johnny, who was ornery, kept calling Missy "banana legs." Missy was insulted and became hurt and angry, which is just what Johnny wanted, because he was having a good time. So he kept calling her silly names and laughed at her when she reacted. I took Missy aside and advised her to stop letting Johnny bother her, because he was having a good time "getting a rise" out of her. I advised her to totally ignore Johnny and pretend as if she didn't even hear him. When she was able to do this, Johnny stopped, because it wasn't fun to tease her anymore. In a few days they were good friends. Help your child determine if the other person's behavior is meant to be cruel or just for fun. Most of the times, bullying will stop if the victims pretend they don't notice.

Physical Defects

Some children have physical traits, such as large ears, crossed eyes, scars, large birthmarks, or are disabled in some way that particularly attracts the attention of unkind children. ***Teachers and parents must do all they can to protect these children from harassment and ridicule, but there is no way to stop it completely. They must try to teach them to ignore unkind behavior.*** Children with physical defects face a painful childhood of heartache and hurt, not only because they're disabled, but also from the taunting they receive from unkind students. Teachers should come down hard on these bullies and get their parents involved.

Personality Defects

In each classroom there are children who have character and behavior traits that are so gross and totally unacceptable that the other students can't help but be repelled. These poor children are ridiculed and socially unaccepted. Having no friends compounds their problems…they can't possibly concentrate on learning. *Some of the undesirable characteristics they may have are: uncleanliness, a bad odor, nose picking, poor eating habits, and continuous tattling or fighting.* If your child has difficulty making friends or maintaining friendships, there may be a good reason.

You can find out by asking her questions each day about who she played with or sat with for lunch. *Ask the teacher for insight into the possible reasons she has no friends. You must concentrate on helping your child overcome any defects that repel other students.*

Bedwetting

Bedwetting is a problem many children have, yet very little has been said from the teachers' standpoint about the detrimental effect it can have on school children. Some parents seem to regard it as something of which to be ashamed and consequently, their children feel shame and guilt when it happens to them. *With some, bedwetting continues well into the upper elementary grades. Parents must be aware that when the child wets his bed, he doesn't appear to have an odor at home, but in a warm and crowded classroom, the odor is almost unbearable.* Rude students will openly ridicule the offender while others will politely ask the teacher to let them move to another seat, away from the offensive odor. There are a number of reasons why children wet the bed. Some are more complicated than others:

1. Occasionally, there is a physical condition causing the child to wet the bed, which must be determined by the child's pediatrician. If a consistent pattern begins to develop, be certain to have her examine your child and advise you.

2. Ask his doctor to explain the treatment options that are available such as enuresis alarms, medication, and changes in lifestyle. Sometimes medications are prescribed for children older than six.

3. Infrequent episodes may be caused by bad dreams, drinking too much water before bedtime, and excess fatigue upon retiring. These causes are easily overcome.

4. Some children may not want to leave the comfort of their bed or may be afraid

1. of the dark, so they wait too long and eventually wet the bed.
2. More serious underlying fears and stress may be at the root. If this is a possibility, you will have to do some deep searching to find the cause and help the child overcome it. The problem will eventually stop when the child learns how to cope with his problems, but it would be so much better if parents could discover the underlying cause earlier.

Recommendations

- Don't make your child feel ashamed or guilty. Don't scold or humiliate him by calling him a baby, or threaten to put a diaper on him.
- If there are older siblings, don't allow them to make fun of him or call him names.
- Don't make him change his sheets as a punishment. Rather, have him help you change his bed and put his sheets in the wash, or let him do it himself if he's old enough. My two boys wet the bed until they were in fifth grade, and they washed and changed their sheets together.
- Don't let the child go to school without bathing. If there's not enough time, a sponge bath with soap and a washcloth is just as good as a bath.
- Discuss the problem openly with your child. To keep quiet about it is almost as bad as humiliating him. You might as well tell him you're ashamed of him.
- Assure him that bed-wetting is common among school children, especially boys, and there is nothing to be ashamed about. Ask him if he has any insight into why it's happening to him. Discuss all the possible causes and some of the solutions you might try together.
- Encourage him to call you to get up with him at night, in case he's reluctant to get up by himself in the dark. Don't let him think that being afraid of the dark is something of which to be ashamed. Tell him about your fears of the dark when you were his age. Have a night light in each room he must go through to reach the bathroom.
- Restrict water an hour before bedtime. Have him use the bathroom before he goes to bed.
- Teach him to set his mind to awaken when he begins to wet the bed. This is done by saying, or thinking to himself while falling asleep that when he needs to pee, he will awaken immediately.
- Assure your child that his wetting the bed won't happen all the time...that he's just going through a temporary stage. Let him know that this happens to many

- other children as well. This kind of reassurance may be more helpful than anything else, since worry, shame, and fear of wetting the bed, even before it happens, may actually cause it to happen.

Overweight Children

One out of three children, ages 2 to 19, in the United States is obese or overweight. These children are extremely unhappy. They have a particularly difficult time overcoming ridicule and are almost always the object of cruel remarks. Abusive students are drawn toward the overweight child. When the fat child is made fun of almost daily, year after year, and there is nothing she can do about it, she will have severe self-esteem problems that may affect her for the rest of her life.

Occasionally, obesity is caused by medical conditions; however, most often the causal factors come directly from the families' eating habits and living style. Usually the parents are also overweight. *One of the worst things parents do to their children is allow them to become overweight. This is the beginning of a lifetime of unhappiness and poor health.* It's really sad to see. If your child is overweight, first get the advice of her pediatrician. If there is nothing physically wrong with her, then get a nutritionist to put her on a healthy diet.

Wise parents will prevent future problems with an overweight child by building the mental and physical health of their family around top nutrition and exercise. I'm sorry to be so harsh on parents in this matter, but *usually, when a child is overweight, it is the parents' fault and they must be blamed for the child's unhappiness.* Following are a number of recommendations by leading health experts:

- Learn about nutrition and cook healthful meals daily.
- Make fat and sugar control a major part of your family's eating habits beginning when your children are infants.
- Often discuss with your child the bad effects junk foods have on her body. Emphasize "You are what you eat."
- Emphasize the importance of drinking four to six glasses of water daily. Don't purchase unhealthful beverages such as colas or artificial juices and punch. These are filled with sugar and caffeine and loaded with calories, and are detrimental to your child's health. If you have them around, your child will drink them. Make them an exception, such as with pizza, hot dogs, or on a picnic.
- Don't purchase unhealthy foods, such as candy, chips, pretzels, or others high

- in fat and calories. These provide little nutrition and are not only conducive to obesity, but also lead to high cholesterol and high blood pressure in the adult years, not to mention cancer and other serious illnesses.
- Explain addiction to your child. Sugar is truly an addiction and it's the parents' job to help their child recognize it.
- Children need snacks and will choose what is available. The first things they will grab are the unhealthy foods, because they taste better. If you don't have them around, they won't eat or drink them. Provide foods such as carrot sticks, celery, fruit, raisins, dried fruit, bread, peanut butter, and healthy smoothies. Look on the Internet for healthy deserts to make.
- For deserts, concentrate on Jell-O, low-cal puddings, and fruits. Make foods like pies, and cakes special occasion deserts. Cookies should have some nutritional value such as raisins, oatmeal, peanut butter, and bran. Always buy low fat and low sugar ice cream.

Family Exercise

Proper nutrition is only one part of having a healthy body and mind; the other is exercise. Most young children love activity, and would naturally get enough exercise, especially if they're athletic and drawn towards sports. However, when they are allowed to sit passively for hours in front of the television while eating chips and drinking soft drinks, the calories that their bodies normally burn off playing are stored as fat, which builds up until they are overweight.

- ***Once again, turn off the television set.*** Don't waste time in front of the idiot tube when you could be at the athletic club, or out walking or riding bikes as a family. Give your child a good example by being actively involved in your own physical exercise program.

- Enroll children in dancing and aerobic classes. Encourage them to participate in athletic activities such as tennis, track, swimming, volleyball, basketball, or softball.
- For family entertainment ride bicycles, walk, dance, jog, swim, roller blade, play tennis, Frisbee, or hike mountain trails together.

It's easier to encourage your family to move more when you move with them. Your family may be walkers. Go for a walk every night after dinner. Or maybe you're runners, or basketball players, or really have no preference at all and just want to try a new form of fitness every day. Take the time to learn what activities your family enjoys together and plan those activities into your day.

Parents serve as role models, not only through direct interaction with their children, but also through the examples they set with their attitude and behavior toward healthy eating and physical activity. Your actions impact how your child thinks and feels about fitness. If you care about your child's health, then focus on your own health and be the role model that sets the pace for your family's healthy choices

Studies have shown that much of the learning that occurs during our children's development is gained through observation and imitation. Our kids are more likely to imitate us if we spend time with them and are intentional about the example we are setting. As parents we can start instilling healthy habits in our kids by adopting healthy habits ourselves. This will give us the credibility we need to lead our children in the healthiest ways.

Dear Parents,

As we come to the end of this book I am engulfed with a warm feeling throughout my entire being. My goal, begun 30 years ago, of showing parents how to help their child become all that he or she can be, has finally reached its end. I did the best I could...the rest is up to you.

I hope that besides helping you gain specific knowledge about the many ways you can help your child, I have also helped you come to certain conclusions. First, that your child, too, can be a top student, given the proper assistance and learning conditions. Second, that you are your child's most important teacher and advocate. No one can ever take your place. And third, you don't have to be wealthy or educated to give your child the best start in life. The most important ingredients are your love, your time, and the desire to do the best you can.

Remember that your child's education is not a destination, but a lifelong journey, which you are obliged to help him travel. Never give up on your duty to your child or the role God has placed you in. I know He will sustain you in this vital role.

I sincerely wish you and your children the greatest happiness and success that education can bring.

God Bless......

Kathleen

Bibliography

Adams, James L., *The Care and Feeding of Ideas*, Wesley, Addison, 1993

Bloom, Benjamin S., *All Our Children Learning*, New York, McGraw Hill Book, 1981

Boegehold, Betty D., *Getting Ready to Read*, Baltimore Books, Maryland, 1984
    Cataldo, Christine Z., *Infant and Toddler Programs*, Reading, Massachusetts, A,
Addison-Wesley Pub. Co, 1983

Caven, Dr. Louise, *The Winning Family: Increasing Self-Esteem in children and
    Yourself*, Nevada, Celestial Arts, 1992

Cutchlow, Tracy, Zero to Five, Washington, Pear Press, 2014

Devine Monica, *Baby Talk, The Art of Communicating with Infants and Toddlers*,
    Masschesetts, Plenam Press, 1991

Dobson, Linda, *The Ultimate Book of Home Schooling*, New York, Three Rivers Press,
    2002

Ginott, Dr., Hairn G., *Between Parent and Child*, New York, MacMillan,1965, *(Revised
    and Updated)* by Ginott, Dr. Alice, and Goddard, Dr. H. Wallace, New York, Three
    Rivers Press, 2003

Gould, Toni S., *Get Ready to Read: A Practical Guide for Teaching Young Children at
    Home and in School*, New York City, Walker, 1991

Graves, Ruth, *The RIF Guide to Encouraging Young Readers*, First Edition, Garden City
    New York, Doubleday, 1987

Rice, Mary F., and Flatter, Charles H., *Help Me Lean, A Handbook for Teaching
    Children from Birth to Third Grade*, Prentice Hall, 1979

Hart, Betty, and Risley, Todd R., *Meaningful Differences in the Everyday Experience of
    Young American Children*, Maryland, Paul H. Brooks Pub. Co., 1995

Hart, Dr. Louise, *The Winning Family: Increasing Self-Esteem in Your Children and
    Yourself*, Celestial Arts, 1993

Hirsch, E.D., Jr and Holdren, John, *What Your Kindergartener Needs to Know*,
    Delta, 1997

Jones, Claudia, *Parents Are Teachers, Too*, VT, Williamson Publishing Co., 1988

Kaye, Peggy, Games for Learning, Farrar, Sraus, Giroux, 1991

Kropp, Paul, Raising a Reader, New York, Doubleday, 1996

Martin, Dr. Grant, Help! My Child Isn't Learning, Colorado Springs, CO 1995

McEwan, Elain, Will My Child Be Ready for School?, Colorado Springs, CO., David C. Cook Publishing Co. 1990

Medina, Dr. John, Brain Rules for Baby, USA, Pear Press, 2011

Meyer, Mary, Ph.D., and Robison, Jennifer, Strengths and Parenting, New York, Gallup Press, 2016

Miller, Karen, Things to Do With toddlers and Twos, Teleshare Publishing Company, Inc. 1984

Pasek, Kathy Hirsh, Ph., D., Michnick, Roberta, Golinkoff, Ph., D., Eyer, Dicha W. Einstein Never Used Flash Cards, New York, Rodale, Inc., 2004

Rath, Linda K., Between the Lions Book for Parents, NY, Harper Collins,2005
Rimms, Dr. Sylvia, Smart Parenting, New York, Three Rivers Pub. Co., 1996iegel, Daniel, Bryson, Tina Payne, The Whole Brain Child, Random House, New York, 2011Sharpe, Wesley, ABC's of School Success, Ed D. Revell, MI, 2005

Shore, Rima, Rethinking the Brain, New Insights into Early Development, Families and Work Institute, 1997

Tracy, Brian, Psychology of Achievement

Trelease, John, The New Read-loud Handbook, 1989,

White, Burton L., Educating the Infant and Toddler, D.C., Heath and Company, 1988

White, Burton L., Kaban, Barbara T., and Attanucci, Jane S., The Origins of Human Competence; The Final Report of the Harvard Preschool Project, Lexington, MA, Lexington Books, 1979

White, Burton L., The First Three Years of Life, NJ, Prentice-Hall, Inc, 1980

Wiener, Harvey S., Ph. D., Any Child Can Read Better, Bantam Books, 1990

Wiener, Harvey S., Ph. D., Any Child Can Write, 1990, New York, Bantam Books, 1990

Wolfgang, Mary E., and Mulle, Corinne, I'm Ready to Learn: Activities for Preschool and Kindergarten Children, Malvern PA, McGraw Hill, 19893

Walsh, David, Smart Parenting, Smarter Kids, New York, N.Y., Free Press, 2011

RECOMMENDED READING

PRESCHOOL

The Very Hungry Caterpillar, by Eric Carle
Alexander and the Wind-Up Mouse, by Leo Lionni
Brown Bear, Brown Bear, What do you See?, by Eric Car
Curious George Series by, H.A. Rey and M.Rey
Dear Zoo, by Rod Campbell
Dino Series by Lisa Wheeler
Don't Let the Pigeon Drive, by Mo Willem
Goodnight Moon, by Margaret Wise Brown
If You Give a Mouse a Cookie, by Laura Numeroff
If You Give a Moose a Muffin, by Laura Numeroff
If You Give a Pig a Pancake, by Laura Numeroff
Is Your Mama a Llama?, by Deborah Guarino
Max's Bath, by Rosemary Wells
Moo, Baa, La La , by Sandra Boynton
Ten in a Bed, by Jan Ormerod
The Cow Loves Cookies, by Karma Wilson
The Monster at the End of this Book, by Jon Stone
The Velveteen Rabbit, by Margery Williams

Friends Through Sand and Stone: Social Skills for Kids on Forgiveness and Friendship, by A. M. Marcus

The Shyness Breakthrough: A No-Stress Plan to Help Your Shy Child Warm Up, Open Up, and Join The Fun, by Bernardo Carducci

104 Activities that Build Self-Esteem teamwork, Communication, Anger Management, Self Discovery, by Alanna Jones

BEGINNNG READERS *(Ages 5 to 8)*

Amelia Bedelia, by Peggy Parrish
Zoobreak, by Gordon Korman
Dr. Seuss, by Theodor Geisel
Beezus and Ramona, by Beverly Clearly
Henry and Ribs, by Beverly Clearly
Where the Wild Things Are, by Maurice Sendak
In the Night Kitchen, by Maurice Sendak
Junie B. Jones Series, by Barbara Park
Winnie-the-Pooh Books, by A.A. Milne
Ivy and Bean Series, by Annie Barrrows
Frog and Toad Books, by Arnold Lobel

CHAPTER BOOKS   8 TO 10

James and the Giant Peach, by RonaldDahl
Charlie and the Chocolate Factory, by Ronald Dahl
Chronicles of Narnia, by C.S. Lewis
Baby Mouse Novels, by Matthew, Jennifer Holm
Percy Jackson Series, by Rick Riordan
Captain Underpants Series, by Dav Pilkey
Diary of a Wimpy Kid Series, by Jeff Kinney
Big Nate Series, by Lincoln Peirce
Dork Diaries Series, by Rachel Renee Russell
Where the Sidewalk Ends, by Shel Silverstein,
Magic Tree House Series, Mary Pope Osborne
A Series of Unfortunate Events, by Lemony Snicket
The Grave Yard Boo, by *Neil Gaiman* novels
Tales of a Fourth-Grade Nothing, byJudy Blume

CLASSICS (ages 10 to 12

Harry Potter Series, by J. K. Rowling
Lord of the Rings Trilogy, by J.R.R. Tolkien
The Hobbit, by J.R.R. Tolkien
The Wizard of Oz, by L. Frank Baum
Little Women, by Louisa May Alcot

Anne of Green Gables, by Lucy Maud Montgomery
Treasure Island, by Robert Louis Stevenson
The Secret Garden, by Frances Burnett
A Wrinkle in Time, by Madeleine L. Engle
Lord of the Files, by William Golding
Great Expectations, by Charles Dickens
Of Mice and Men, by John Steinbeck
Black Beauty, by Anna Sewell
Little House Books, by Laura Ingalls Wilder

DINOSAUR JOKES

For approximately eight-to twelve-year-olds. They would have a ball telling these to their school class. They could also make a Dinosaur Scrapbook with pictures and joke captions. Older students would benefit from researching particular dinosaurs and writing several facts about each one. Be sure you help them find dinosaur library books and research dinosaurs on the Internet.

Q. How do you know a dinosaur is in the dryer?
A. The door won't shut.

Q. How can three dinosaurs go out under a tiny umbrella and not get wet?
A. When it's not raining.

Q. What do you feed long dinosaurs?
A. The same as you feed short dinosaurs.

Q. What do you do when you find a dinosaur sleeping under your bed?
A. Find a ladder so you can climb into bed.

Q. Which dinosaur won the beauty contest? contest?
A. Nobody.

Q. What do you feed long dinosaurs?
A. The same as you feed short dinosaurs.

Q. What do you do when you find a dinosaur in your bed?
A. You find another bed to sleep in.

Q.   What time is it when five dinosaurs are chasing you?

A.   Five after one.

Q.   What's the difference between strawberries and
       dinosaurs?

A.   Strawberries are red.

Q.   What does a dinosaur become after it is one year old?

A.   Two years old.

Q.   What did the caterpillar say when the dinosaur
       stepped on him?

A.   Nothing.

Q.   Why did the dinosaur go over the hill?

A.   Because it couldn't go under it.

Q.   Why do dinosaurs eat raw meat?

A.   Because they can't cook.

Q.   How does a dinosaur keep from dying?

A.   He goes to the living room.

Q.   How do you know a dinosaur is under your bed?

A.   Your head hits the ceiling.

Q.   Why do dinosaurs never forget anything?

A.   Because no one ever tells them anything.

Q.   Why does a brontosaurus have such a
       long neck?

A.   Because its head is so far from its body.

Girl Dino:	Why do you have your leg in a cast?
Boy Dino:	Because I broke it in three places.
Girl Dino:	You shouldn't go to those places anymore.

Mother Dino:	What are you doing?
Baby Dino:	Chasing cavemen.
Mother Dino:	How often do I have to tell you not to play with your food?

Boy Dino:	How do you shoot a blue dinosaur?
Girl Dino:	I don't know.
Boy Dino:	With a blue gun.

Boy Dino:	How do you shoot a white dinosaur?
Girl Dino:	With a white gun.
Boy Dino:	No. You hold its nose until it turns blue, then shoot it with a blue gun.

TOP STUDENTS / TOP PARENTS

**Scientific research leaves no doubt of the impact of
parental influence on the child's overall development:**

The critical learning period for children is between the ages of 8 and 18 months. By the time children are 8 years old they are already set in molds that determine their academic futures, whether they be of success or failure.

The brain can be helped to overcome inexperience or to improve development; however, the most impressionable time for change is within the first 10 years. There is no certain way to increase children's total learning ability without comprehensive effort.

High quality childcare, early education and social contacts provide a lasting impact on children's intelligence and ability to learn; however, most American preschool children who are in day care are in facilities of poor to mediocre quality.

The older the child becomes, the more difficult it is to help him overcome the lack of proper education and stimulation during his preschool years. If parents don't provide the necessary experiences during these crucial years, the best that educators can do is to prepare the children for unskilled jobs.

The amount of language spoken directly to children during their first 3 years is critical to their intellectual development and ability to learn. Parents who talk a lot, give much feedback and approval, ask questions, and give lengthy explanations, will significantly increase their child's I.Q.

Teachers say most children are sent to school unprepared to learn. School for many of these children is the beginning of a lifetime of failure. If preschool children are not prepared for school learning, none of our strategies for teaching them will be as effective.

Parents' education, race, or economic status are irrelevant to a child's healthy and intellectual development. What matters most is the kinds of experiences they provide using language and vocabulary, explanations and conversations, and good role modeling.

The most dominant environmental factor in the life of the child is the mother. She influences her child's experiences more than any other person or circumstances.

CPSIA information can be obtained
at www.ICGtesting.com
Printed in the USA
LVHW101617170321
681769LV00005B/323